CHAI C

Bishwanath Ghosh, born in Kanpur on 26 December 1970, is the author of the hugely popular *Aimless in Banaras: Wanderings in India's Holiest City*. He's also a Hindi poet, who has two well-received compilations—*Jiyo Banaras* and *Tedhi-Medhi Lakeeren*—to his credit. His other books include *Tamarind City: Where Modern India Began*; *Longing, Belonging: An Outsider at Home in Calcutta*; and *Gazing at Neighbours: Travels Along the Line that Partitioned India*. He is an Associate Editor with *The Hindu* newspaper and lives in Calcutta.

Praise for *Chai, Chai*

'Author Bishwanath Ghosh writes *Chai, Chai* with the enthusiasm of an explorer, painting a rather adventurous picture of days spent in these seemingly non-destination towns.' – *Business Standard*

'The story of *Chai, Chai* is in the details that the writer has registered in simple, lucid prose.' – *India Today, Travel Plus*

'One of the most delightful books I have read.' – Mahesh Dattani

'*Chai, Chai* makes for effortless reading.' – *The Hindu*

'What works for Ghosh is his power of observation.' – *Deccan Herald*

'Precise details make all the difference.' – Eunice De Souza, *Mumbai Mirror*

ALSO BY BISHWANATH GHOSH

Tamarind City: Where Modern India Began (2012)
Longing, Belonging: An Outsider at Home in Calcutta (2014)
Gazing at Neighbours: Travels Along the Lines that Partitioned India (2017)
Aimless in Banaras: Wanderings in India's Holiest City (2019)

BISHWANATH GHOSH

CHAI CHAI

TRAVELS IN PLACES WHERE YOU STOP BUT NEVER GET OFF

First published by Tranquebar, an imprint of westland ltd, in 2009

Published by Tranquebar, an imprint of Westland Books, a division of Nasadiya Technologies Private Limited, in 2022

No. 269/2B, First Floor, 'Irai Arul', Vimalraj Street, Nethaji Nagar, Allappakkam Main Road, Maduravoyal, Chennai 600095

Westland, the Westland logo, Tranquebar and the Tranquebar logo are the trademarks of Nasadiya Technologies Private Limited, or its affiliates.

Copyright © Bishwanath Ghosh, 2009

Bishwanath Ghosh asserts the moral right to be identified as the author of this work.

ISBN: 9789395073219

10 9 8 7 6 5 4 3 2

The views and opinions expressed in this work are the author's own and the facts are as reported by him, and the publisher is in no way liable for the same.

All rights reserved

Typeset by SÜRYA, New Delhi
Printed at Saurabh Printers Pvt. Ltd.

No part of this book may be reproduced, or stored in a retrieval system, or transmitted in any form or by any means, electronic, mechanical, photocopying, recording, or otherwise, without express written permission of the publisher.

For my parents,
Karabi and Samir Ghosh

CONTENTS

Author's Note	ix
PROLOGUE	
Tiny Towns: Jumbo Junctions	1
TRAIN TO CHILDHOOD	
Mughal Sarai	7
KAMA COUNTRY BECKONS	
Jhansi	56
NAVEL OF INDIA	
Itarsi	95
FROZEN IN TIME	
Guntakal	136
TOUCH AND GO	
Arakkonam and Jolarpettai	172
BY THE BHARATHAPUZHA	
Shoranur	189
Acknowledgements	212

Places remembered

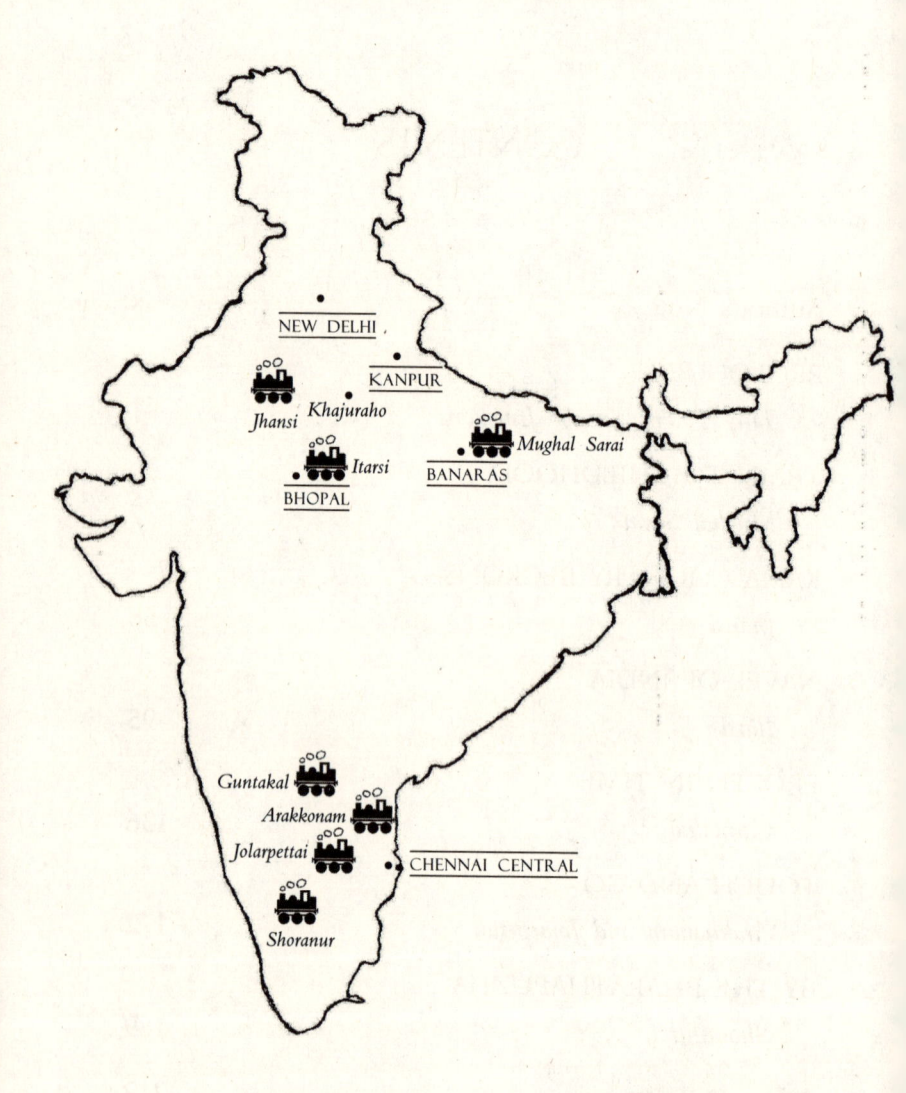

Map not to scale

AUTHOR'S NOTE

REFLECTIONS ON THE BOOK

THE PRINT ORDER FOR *Chai, Chai*, when it was published in the autumn of 2009, was 2,000 copies. One evening, shortly before it was to hit the stands, I was having a drink with an editor, a genuine well-wisher, who expressed concern as to whether I would be able to sell those many copies.

The concern wasn't unfounded: books don't sell easily in India, unless they happen to be works of established authors or are cheaply priced for mass reading. '*Roti, kapdaa aur makaan*'—food, clothing and shelter—'these are the top priorities of Indians,' the editor had said. 'Buying books figures way below in the list.'

I wasn't too worried, however. I did not have a reputation to defend, nor was I expecting to make money from the book. At least I got to travel to new places—at the expense of my publisher.

Chai, Chai, as it turned out, went for a reprint within three weeks of its publication. Ever since then—it's been five years now—the book has gone into several reprints and I can now see why.

The romance of the railways is too deep-rooted in the Indian consciousness to go stale even in the time of budget airlines. The sight of a train, the scenes from the train window, the unexpected halt at a small station in the middle of nowhere, the arrival at the destination—they still bring out the child in us.

Railways is not all romance, it is a reality. More people are taking the train than ever before. Try booking seats online and you will find all the seats taken for the next several weeks—no matter which train or what destination. More trains are introduced every year, stations are upgraded, more facilities provided to passengers. If anything, it is the number of airlines that appears to be shrinking.

The curiosity is, therefore, inherent: to read about trains, about the places they take you to—and about the places they take you through. The places they take you through—the vast fields, the villages, the small towns, often represented by a railway junction—is where the real India lives. *Chai, Chai* celebrates these junctions.

While on the one hand it is gratifying to see the book doing well, on the other, there is also a regret that I will always nurse. When I was visiting Mughal Sarai to gather material for the book, I also happened to travel to Benares, which is just ten kilometres away. As I roamed the streets of what is considered India's oldest and holiest city, I was struck by the sight of the countless funeral processions converging on its ghats. This was November 2007. Little did I know that, less than two years later, I would be back in Benares to lend a shoulder to the string cot carrying my mother's body.

Unlike many other people who choose to die in

Benares or wish to be cremated there, my mother only happened to be in Benares. She and my father were visiting my brother, who lived there at the time, when she died suddenly, at the age of fifty-nine. After her cremation, we took the train to Kanpur, our home, where my brother and I observed the customary thirteen-day mourning by not shaving and remaining barefoot and eating only bland food. It was during this period, eight days after my mother's death, that a courier delivered home the first copy of *Chai, Chai*. She had just missed seeing her son's debut work.

CHAI, CHAI WAS TREATED with kindness by most reviewers, but there is one recurring complaint I keep receiving about it, even from those who have liked the book: that it contains too many episodes of my drinking in the local bars.

I can only say that I was trying to be faithful to the narrative, describing things as they happened to me, without deliberately leaving out certain experiences and magnifying certain others. That was a time when I looked forward to having a drink or three, even during the day—a hangover from my years in Delhi where, at the Press Club, lunch would invariably be preceded by two rounds of vodka.

Also, in the small towns that are described in the book, there is very little for a visitor to do once the sun has set. You either retire to your lodge and watch TV, if at all it has a TV, or go to the nearest watering hole, where all the action is. Bars are where strangers open up and talk, and where you most often get the flavour of the town.

Today, if I were to write *Chai, Chai* all over again, I would do it differently. I can already imagine it being written differently, and what I see is a work that is laboured and trying to impress. Whereas the book you are holding in your hands is raw. I can rewrite the prose, but I cannot replicate its energy.

BG
November 2014

PROLOGUE
TINY TOWNS, JUMBO JUNCTIONS

RAILWAY STATIONS IN INDIA stand like fiercely-independent states within cities and towns, insulated from the local flavour, as if they are territories of a common colonial master sitting in Delhi, which they are anyway.

Such is their sameness that if you were to ignore the yellow slab and all other signboards that identify a railway station, you would barely know where you are. All you would know is that you are in a country where tea is available round the clock and whose inhabitants have two primary occupations—travelling and waiting.

If you have been waiting for a while, you might find a clue about your location though—when the vendors yell at each other in the local language, or when an announcement on the PA system comes up. If the announcement is made in Tamil, apart from the standard Hindi and English, you know you are in Tamil Nadu. But where exactly in Tamil Nadu? It could be Madurai or Coimbatore. As cities, each of them has a distinct identity. But sitting inside the railway station, it would be almost impossible to tell one from the other.

And when you are travelling in a long-distance train like the Tamil Nadu Express, it is often not possible to tell Tamil Nadu from Andhra Pradesh, or Andhra Pradesh from Maharashtra. You would have to rely on the chaiwallah to tell you your current location, in case you have missed the yellow signboard.

India can have no better symbol for national integration than the railways. The railway reservation form does not ask you anything other than your name, age, gender and address. In trains, people of two castes who would otherwise not like to be seen in each other's company, cohabit without fuss for hours, even a couple of days. A millionaire who travels in a first-class air-conditioned compartment to maintain his exclusivity is forced to share the makeshift bedroom with a much poorer countryman who happens to be travelling on office expense. In the air-conditioned coupe, they are equals: the rich man putting up with the snoring of the poor.

The journeys are not just about the levelling, but also about getting acquainted with each other's cultures, especially food habits. Marwaris, when they travel as a large family, carry a stock of food that would last them the journey. The piles of *puris* are in proportion to the number of travelling members, the eating capacity of each member, and the number of meals they would have on the train. Just when you are hungry and waiting for the pantry-car boy to deliver your meal, you find them taking the lid off their food basket and releasing into the compartment the delicious whiff of *puri*, *sabzi* and pickles.

It is the youngest of the women who usually opens the basket. The men, starting with the eldest, are served first. At times there are so many *puris* being passed around that I have felt tempted to ask, 'Can I have a couple of them, please?'

Tamil families usually carry their stock as well: *idlis* and an oily paste of what they call the chutney powder. The *idli* has always been my weakness, and I have always imagined the round, steel tiffin-box being extended to me: 'Mind having one?' But I have always looked away while the steel box is being passed around. Bengalis, on the other hand, rarely carry food: for them, the train journey is another excuse to eat out. After eating, they would compare if the chicken curry was as good as the one served on Rajdhani Express six months ago. Most often it isn't, but that's a different story. The story here is that the railways are not just a means of transport, but the circulatory system of India. No railways, no India.

But not many spare a thought for the arterial valves that pump the blood: the big junctions which facilitate the movement of trains from one corner of India to the other. These are stations where, for decades, trains have been making long, rejuvenating stops so that engines could be changed and the coaches cleaned and the food loaded.

For travel-weary passengers, the long halt meant a chance to stretch their legs on the platform and refill water and have tea. Or buy cigarettes or newspapers or the latest issue of *Stardust*. Or even saunter out of the station to buy a bottle of beer: the train wasn't going to leave anytime soon.

Over the years, these junctions have become a landmark

in the lives of long-distance passengers—even for those who would have spent hours sitting on their benches, waiting for the connecting train to their destination, because many cities were not directly linked until fairly recently.

For example, there was no direct train from Bangalore to Bombay until the late 1970s. Passengers from Bangalore had to wait for hours at Guntakal, in Andhra Pradesh, for the connecting train to Bombay which came from Madras. Similarly, those wanting to travel from Lucknow to any city in south India, be it Madras or Trivandrum, had to spend a better part of the day at Jhansi station to catch the connecting train. For such passengers, these junctions are now part of their personal history.

Yet these junctions, even though they bind the extreme corners of India, are hardly ever mentioned other than in the context of train travel. That is because as towns, they are too small to matter to you. They too must be having stories to tell—just that nobody ever steps out of the station yard to listen.

THE IDEA FOR THIS BOOK took root one evening two years ago, when, travelling in the Gorakhpur–Trivandrum Express, I had stepped out of the train at Itarsi station to stretch my legs and have a cup of tea. I was returning from Kanpur, my hometown, to Madras, where I now live. Twelve hours of journey was behind me, and twenty-four were still to go. There were people in the train who had boarded ten hours before me, and would be travelling for fifteen hours more after I got down. The train, after all, connects the Himalayas to the Indian Ocean.

If you were a research scholar assigned to grade the Indian states based on the public behaviour of their people, the wisest thing would be to travel second class on a train like this, right from Gorakhpur to Trivandrum. In the beginning, you will travel in an India where might is right. The 'daily passengers'—office-goers and students who travel to nearby towns daily to work or study—will make you feel as if your seat rightfully belongs to them. You will be required to shrink on your seat to give them space. The land you are passing through, after all, belongs to them. Towards the end of the journey, however, you will encounter an entirely different kind of 'daily passengers'—shy Malayali men and women who try very hard not to invade your privacy.

The reversal of 'might is right' begins at Itarsi, a big railway junction in Madhya Pradesh. It is a small town seated at the foot of the Vindhyas—the mountain range that effectively divides India into north and south.

Most trains have a longish halt at Itarsi. That evening, as soon as I had stepped onto the platform, I realised I had one final chance to treat myself to north Indian snacks: by the next morning, even the snacks would have become south Indian in character. Therefore, I bought two *alu bondas*, served on a piece of paper along with a pair of green chillies.

As I stood on the platform, eating the *bondas* and washing them down with railway-station tea, the familiar female voice relentlessly announced the arrivals or delays of various trains. During those few minutes that I had spent on the platform, I had heard names of stations from every corner of India being mentioned over the PA system: Amritsar, Bombay, Guwahati, Trivandrum, Howrah, Chennai.

It then struck me that nearly all trains running across the length and breadth of the country—Bombay to Calcutta, Delhi to Madras, Kochi to Guwahati, Ahmedabad to Hyderabad, and so on—will have to pass through Itarsi. If someone were to blow up the rail tracks at Itarsi junction, the country would plunge into chaos for several days—so crucial is its location on the railway map.

Yet, Itarsi is almost non-existent in our daily life. You are unlikely to have come across someone who works in Itarsi. You are unlikely to have ever posted a letter that bears an Itarsi address. Itarsi is only thought of as a railway station, where you get down and have tea and something to eat, and then move on. How does Itarsi, the town, look like?

Similarly, the mention of Mughal Sarai will only conjure up, in the mind of a Bengali or a Bihari, the image of a busy railway station, just as Jolarpet will for a Tamilian or a Malayali travelling regularly within the south. They will find it impossible to imagine these places as populated towns where people go about their daily lives just like people do elsewhere. That's because these places have never been their destination, but only the gateways to their destination.

Why not, then, get off at these junctions for a change, and wander out of the station yard into the towns and listen to the stories they might be waiting to tell—instead of just standing on the platform and looking out for the man calling, '*Chai! Chai!*'

TRAIN TO CHILDHOOD
MUGHAL SARAI

AT FOUR IN THE chilly morning, the town of Mughal Sarai was fast asleep. Not a soul in sight as the rickshaw-puller took me to a hotel that was supposed to be two kilometres from the station.

I should have felt important. It is not very often that you find yourself to be the sole commuter on the 500-year-old Grand Trunk Road—the lifeline of India, the highway of the Hindi heartland, the tar thread that runs along the Gangetic Plain to connect Punjabi aggression with Bengali intellect.

But I was nervous. I had heard only unflattering things about Mughal Sarai. An editor, who had never been there, told me the place was crime-ridden. A police constable, who had lived there, warned me that the place was infested with *goondas*. And now I was right there, at this vulnerable hour, completely at the mercy of a town that sat on the eastern edge of Uttar Pradesh, dangerously close to Bihar.

I had been desperately hoping that the train would bring me to Mughal Sarai well after sunrise. But when you are too eager to avoid a situation, you invariably end up stepping on its tail, just the way I had stepped onto the platform—at 3.15 in the morning.

Until twenty-five years ago, the same town was a source of fascination for me rather than fear: the train would make an interminably long halt here during our annual trips from Kanpur to Calcutta. It was here that lunch would be served, in compartmented aluminium trays, along with tepid water that came in glass bottles with no crown or cap.

I had wanted to linger in the station till daybreak, when it might have been safer to venture into the town. To while away time I had bought tea and sat on a bench occupied partly by a dozing elderly couple. The platform resembled a large ward of a government hospital, with dozens of people scattered around on improvised beds—on the floor, by the walls, on the benches. They all looked numbed and weary, as if reeling under an epidemic or a natural calamity. Then I bought some more tea—the *chaiwallah* was pouring it into clay cups—and a Hindi newspaper, and then killed some more time strolling up and down the platform. But the station clock moved too slowly for my comfort. I had run out of patience and headed for the exit, where I found a swarm of rickshaw pullers and taxi drivers waiting to embrace me like long-lost relatives.

'*Saahab, kahaan jaana hai?*'—Sir, where do you want to go?

I had no idea myself, and telling them that could have meant trouble. So I had waved them off and looked at my watch repeatedly with mock impatience, as if a vehicle was on its way to fetch me. I was cold and hungry, and my bones were aching for a comfortable bed.

When I could no longer wait for the imaginary car, I had ended up asking a taxi driver if he could suggest me a good hotel. He did suggest one, a hotel called Saraswati, only two kilometres away. To my surprise, he had not offered to take me there. Clearly, he had no vested interest, and that had made me take his recommendation seriously. So I had hailed a cycle-rickshaw.

And right now, with the bustle of the station behind me, I was out on the deserted road, where the only other form of life I saw was three stray dogs hovering around the mortal remains of a companion who must have been knocked down by a truck a few hours before. And the only other human form I saw was on the giant poster of a Bhojpuri film, *Kab Aibu Anganwaa Hamaar?*—When will you come to my courtyard? In the Hindi heartland, inviting a woman to your courtyard is an indirect way of proposing to her.

In the pre-dawn hours, no matter where you live, the air is always laden with a smell that I have always found impossible to describe. Right now that smell and the silence were reminding me of school days when I would wake up—rather, would be woken up—at four every morning. It is supposed to be the best time to study, but back then you envied people in the family who could afford to sleep on beyond four. Today, after years of being habituated to going to sleep only around four, I had been woken up at that hour by the attendant in the train. Like Mughal Sarai, another lost piece of childhood was catching up.

At Hotel Saraswati, I was hoping to walk into a reception area where the sleepy manager would first relieve my shoulder of the various bags and then embrace me for having set foot on Mughal Sarai. But I found the entrance, a collapsible gate, locked from inside. I rang the bell twice. No response. I returned to the rickshaw-puller and asked him to take me back to the station.

He said, '*Ek baar ghanta aur bajaiye*'—Ring the bell once more.

I walked back and pressed the switch again. From the corner of the building a window opened and a head popped out.

'*Kya chahiye?*'—What do you want?

'*Kamraa chahiye*'—I want a room.

'*Koi kamraa khaali nahi hai*'—No room is vacant.

The window shut.

Once again, I became a child of the Grand Trunk Road. Still not a soul in sight as we headed back to the station.

I tried making conversation with the rickshaw-puller, but he was in no mood to indulge me. I was a burden for him now: being his passenger, I had failed to find a room in the hotel he had taken me to, and now it was his moral obligation to find me accommodation at this hour, but he didn't seem to know of any other place. All he could do now was deposit me back at the station, but then, would I pay him what he was expecting, considering the journey had turned out to be futile? The question must have weighed heavily on his mind as he pedalled me back without a word.

Only after I paid him what he asked for—twenty rupees—that he smiled and even offered to wait while I looked for hotels around the station. I could spot only one multi-storey hotel outside the station and considering that its signboard was illuminated by a neon light, it seemed the kind that would offer some comfort on a chilly November morning. I cursed myself for not having tried my luck at this place before (I had noticed the neon signboard from the station). But here too, a lock was hanging from the collapsible gate. As I looked for a bell, a man emerged from the shadows.

'What do you want?' he asked rather rudely.

'A room,' I replied.

'All rooms are full,' he said abruptly and disappeared into the darkness he had appeared from. The sun showed no signs of rising. Only the railway station was wide awake at this hour, apart from the taxi drivers and the rickshaw-pullers. As I stood there, clueless about what to do next, I could hear the familiar announcements emanating from the station, '*Yaatrigan kripaya dhyaan dijiye*'—Passengers, your kind attention please.

My rickshaw-puller was still standing there, more clueless than I was. So I hired another, who berated the previous one, 'Why pull a rickshaw in Mughal Sarai if you can't find sir a hotel?' Saying this, the new man took off, and I found myself back on the Grand Trunk Road.

Soon he took a turn and we entered a dark, narrow, cobbled street. In the little light, I could only see downed shutters on either side. The rickshaw tyres made so much noise on the stones that I was worried about waking people up. And they need not be the nice sort.

The rickshaw-puller brought me to a building which, once again, had a collapsible gate with a lock hanging from inside. He asked me to read the signboard. It said: Devi Lodge.

When I asked him why he wanted me to read it, he said, '*Babu*, I am illiterate. I can't read or write. So I was wondering if I have brought you to the right place.'

'But the gate is locked,' I told him.

'Don't worry,' he said and climbed down from the rickshaw and thumped on the gate.

A tubby, *lungi*-clad man appeared, rubbing his eyes. He looked irritated. The rickshaw-puller said, '*Saahab ko kamraa chahiye*'—Sir wants a room.

The *lungi*-clad man opened the lock rather reluctantly and let me in. I told him I wanted the best room. He thought for a while and said, 'Fine, but it will cost you Rs 180 a day.' Upon hearing this, my head told me to return to the rickshaw right away, but my hand was already writing on a register that asked my name, address, nationality, where I had come from, where I was headed to, the nature of my visit and so on.

As I paid him an advance of Rs 200, I heard the rickshaw-puller murmur about his commission for getting me here. The *lungi*-clad man nodded and waved him away. Precisely at this moment, power went off and I found myself in total darkness.

'Load shedding,' I heard the man curse in the dark. After that, there was complete silence. In tense moments like these, the sadist in you waits rather gleefully to see what happens next, especially when you choose to invite such tense moments upon yourself.

Before I could reflect upon my fate a thin candle lit up, illuminating the face of the man. 'Power goes off every morning at six. Now it will come back only at ten. Come, I will show you the room.'

Following him in the candlelight, I climbed a narrow

staircase that smelt as if no one had preceded me on it for decades. The smell could have been that of the man's mind: 'Ah, finally we got hold of a customer.' We climbed up to the second floor where he showed me into a room—the best room in that lodge.

I ran my eyes around the room: a double-bed that smelt and looked as if the sheets had not been changed in months and had been vacated only an hour before my arrival; a rickety table in one corner; and even more rickety electrical switches that were of no use now. The drone of the mosquitoes failed to hide a soft, strange sound emanating from the bathroom. When I brought it to the notice of the *lungi*-clad man, he went inside and inspected.

'Oh no, the tap is leaking. I've been telling them to fix it, but who listens?' He fixed the candle on a table and left.

I lay on the bed with my clothes on. There was no question of changing to get into a bed that didn't look or smell good even in candlelight.

If I had interesting company, say someone I happened to befriend in the train after discovering that she, too, was coming to Mughal Sarai to explore the town but had no idea about where to stay, I might have seen things in a different light. But right now I had only murderous mosquitoes and the sound of a leaking tap for company.

I lit a cigarette and went out to the balcony. Spread out mysteriously in front of me was the silhouette of a town that was so integral to my childhood. The annual journeys from Kanpur to Calcutta would not have been half as exciting but for the prolonged halt at Mughal Sarai. The station used to be the recharge point in the days when trains hurtled down the length and breadth of India like a chain of marooned islands, cutting you from the rest of the world till you reached a big junction. Even if the prime minister was shot, you would get to know of it only from the newspaper vendor at the junction.

WHEN I WOKE UP it was eight. I had managed to sleep for two hours. The sunlight made the room look less depressing. I went to the balcony again. The town was no longer mysterious but all too familiar—the buildings whose silhouette I saw a few hours ago could have belonged to a modest neighbourhood in my hometown, Kanpur, or anywhere in north India.

On the terraces of the various houses, women went about their morning chore of washing clothes and spreading them out on nylon ropes—all this under the gaze of men lounging on adjoining terraces with their morning tea. On the terrace right across the lodge appeared a man wearing a towel and carrying his shaving cup: he peeped below, and seeing that no one was passing by, splashed the contents of the cup onto the street.

I had two options now: either go back to sleep or go out in search of food. There was a third option too—to set out for Benares, which was barely ten kilometres away. The thought of food, however, was more appealing and once again I was out on Grand Trunk Road.

Shops were now pulling up their shutters and the pavement had begun to swarm with hawkers who had just spread out their wares: ropes, lanterns, spices, cheap garments—almost every requirement of a small town and the villages around it.

I tried imagining how the place must have looked when Sher Shah Suri—the Bihar-born Afghan warrior-administrator who had displaced Mughal emperor Humayun from his throne for fifteen long years—was laying it in the sixteenth century. The canvas for my imagination was as vast and empty as this place must have been then.

I walked into the first sweetshop-cum-eatery I came across and ordered *puri-sabzi*. In one corner sat an incredibly fat man, who seemed to be on his way to work because he kept looking at his watch. He had already had some *puri*s and waiting for more. 'Do puri aur dijiyega,' he kept shouting—Get me two more *puri*s.

But no one paid attention. The shopkeeper and his minions were busy putting *laddu*s into boxes. The sweets were for a wedding and had to be packed urgently.

The pride of the fat man, who kept looking at his watch, told him that a petty shopkeeper cannot afford to ignore him like this and that he must walk out right away. But his taste buds, already aroused by the first lot of *puri*s, warned him that it would be foolish to abandon such a delicious breakfast just because the shopkeeper is a little busy.

In sheer exasperation, he raised his voice again. He broke into an angry speech and after he was done, he looked at me for a nod of approval: he had noticed that even I had been waiting impatiently for my breakfast.

Before his exasperation could turn into tears, a boy came up and dropped two hot *puri*s on his plate. Overcome by gratification, he also ordered a plate of *jalebi*s. He saw me looking at him and immediately looked away. We were no longer in the same boat: he had got his *puris*, while I was still waiting for mine.

Nothing makes you lust for food more than when you see adjacent tables being served while you know you will have to wait. My *puri-sabzi* came only after the fat man was gone and the shopkeeper had sent off his consignment of *laddu*s.

On the way back to the lodge, I bought Savlon soap along with a cheap T-shirt and *lungi*, which I wanted to wear in bed and leave behind when I left Mughal Sarai. The *lungi*-wearing man who had showed me my room was sitting at the reception. He was now freshly bathed, had changed into shirt and trousers, and was reading the newspaper.

I smiled at him, he smiled back, but not in a very encouraging way. As if he was telling me, 'You mind your business, I will mind mine. Let's not get into a conversation.' This was something unusual in the Hindi heartland, where people look for excuses to open a conversation. I asked him why there were so many beauty parlours in Mughal Sarai: I had counted five of them on that very lane.

At first the man blushed at my question. Then he asked me about my profession. Usually, the mention of the word 'journalist' makes people warm up to you. But this man was still hesitant to talk. I handed him my visiting card again—I had given him one the night before. He scrutinised it. He asked me the purpose of my visit to Mughal Sarai. I told him. He smiled tentatively.

'So you were asking about beauty parlours. *Aaj kal ladies logon ko shringar karne ka shauq hai* (women like to look good these days). There are so many weddings, so many functions, so many parties to attend. Everything is an occasion these days. So it is only natural that they want to look good.'

I knew what he meant. The concept of 'looking good' had percolated, inevitably, to the small town. Why should it be the preserve of the big city anyway? 'Face pack'—a term almost unheard of in India till fifteen years ago—is today as common as toothpaste. Today, even I—a man—might consider getting a facial before a special occasion.

Back in my room I had to make do with Savlon soap, which I rubbed vigorously all over my body to get rid of the germs that I might have acquired from the bed. Then, putting on the T-shirt and *lungi*, I lay down on that bed. The electricity was back and the whirring fan lent a sense of normalcy to the room. After a heavy breakfast of *puris*, it was a good idea to get some sleep. I needed it. Mughal Sarai could wait.

There was very little I knew about Mughal Sarai when I set out on the journey. I only had visions of visiting a crumbling caravanserai that must have throbbed with life during the Mughal era, catering to weary travellers passing by in carts drawn by horses, bullocks and camels.

But no search engine on the Internet mentioned any such inn, or even the remains of it. In fact, the Internet did not provide anything to give me even a remote idea of why the place was named so or what it looked like. All I got to know was that it used to be the biggest railway marshalling yard in Asia and a prominent coal market—and was also the birthplace of India's second prime minister, Lal Bahadur Shastri. No account of the romance associated with the railways. If at all Mughal Sarai is popular on the Internet, it's solely because of its proximity to Benares.

I SLEPT ALL DAY. Woken up by the evening invasion of mosquitoes, I went out for a stroll. The Grand Trunk Road now dazzled brightly enough to catch the attention of an astronaut up in the sky. The dazzle, however, illuminated the unhurried, uncomplicated life that dated back to the days when the spacecraft was not even invented: men with cloth bags going from shop to shop, buying groceries; women bent over fresh piles of vegetables, haggling with the vendors; giggly girls and shy couples feasting on spicy *alu tikki* and *pani puri* from roadside *chaat*-sellers.

The *chaatwallah* is an important person in north India. He adds spice to your mundane life. He represents a break from routine. I surveyed the *chaat*-selling carts and settled for the one that was the busiest. It was run by a middle-aged couple and their son—perhaps grandson. They had their roles cut out. The man prepared the savouries and handed them to the woman on leaf-plates. The woman did the elaborate garnishing before passing on the plates to the waiting customers. The boy's job was to serve *pani puri* and keep an eye on who ate what and how much. It was the boy who told you the bill amount.

My indulgence at the *chaat* stall robbed me of my desire for a drink. But having survived a long rickshaw ride at four in the morning, having survived a room whose depressing interior I would not wish even upon my enemies, having survived the uncertainty of finding an accommodation at all, I was determined to have one, or maybe two.

But where was the bar? Not very far, I discovered. Barely twenty steps away from the *chaatwallah* was a wine shop and in its basement, a bar, whose glass door welcomed me with the sign, 'Wishing You Happy Diwali'.

A typical Indian bar, the one that is attached to a liquor shop, is mainly meant to facilitate clandestine drinking. Since the society looks down upon drinking and the family considers it a taboo, such bars are the only place where you can drink in peace, without burning a hole in your pocket.

In such bars, it is almost obligatory to order some snacks to go with the drink, especially if you want to be treated well by the people who run the bar, because the snacks are their primary source of income. I took a corner table, already occupied by a man, and ordered a quarter-bottle—180 ml—of whisky.

'What about snacks?' the gym-fit waiter asked.

'Nothing,' I said.

'*Kuchh to?*' he persisted—Something at least?

'First get the whisky,' I told him.

While he was gone, I noticed the 'Rate Board':

	Full	*Half*
Chicken fry	Rs 180	Rs 80
Paneer chilli	Rs 60	Rs 30
Chicken chilli	Rs 60	Rs 30
Paneer pakoda	Rs 40	Rs 25
Machhli	Rs 40	Rs 20

I looked at the people around me: many of them appeared to be farmers winding down after a hard day's work. They had *gamchhaas*, thin towels, around their necks—an indication that they possibly belonged to the toiling community.

Most of the noise in the bar was made by the occupants of a table that was closest to the cash counter: four young men who stood out because of their fashionable clothes and who were drinking for fun unlike the others who were mournfully taking sips from their glasses. The noisiest among them was a jolly young Sikh, who seemed to be the source of all the laughter emanating from the table.

The man whose table I shared looked very sad. He drank in total silence. I was tempted to start a conversation, but I needed a drink first. The boy returned with the bottle of whisky, poured my drink and again asked me what I would have for snacks. I knew there was no escape if I had to sit here and enjoy my drink, so I ordered *paneer pakoda*. When the *pakoda*s came, I pushed the plate towards the sad-looking man. He refused at first, but after some goading hesitantly picked up a piece. Soon he began talking.

His name was Babu. He was into the 'marble business'—which meant getting marble slabs fixed in people's kitchens and bathrooms. He was rather happy until a few years ago when labourers charged Rs 30–35 per day for marbling an area of eight to ten square feet. 'But today they charge Rs 80–85 for just five square feet. If we pay the labourers so much, what are we contractors left with? And earlier, only one or two people like me were into this business. Today there are dozens of them. Why should anyone call me?'

His glass was getting empty, and I asked him if he would like to have a drink from my bottle. His eyes shone with lust but his hands rose in Indian politeness, 'No, no, sir.' But he didn't stop me when I took his glass and poured him a drink.

'You can't imagine, sir, how rapidly things are changing. Till the other day, one *bissa* of land here cost Rs 1,600. Today one *bissa* costs Rs 3 lakh. Can you imagine?' I asked him how much a *bissa* was. He thought for a while and then scribbled the converted figure on my notebook: 1365 sq ft.

I asked him about Mughal Sarai—what kind of a place was it? He said he could not imagine earning his living in any other place: he was born here, and he would always live here, come what may.

I asked him whether Mughal Sarai was affected by incidents that aimed to cause communal strife in Benares, such as the blast at the Sankat Mochan temple in early 2006. He answered with an emphatic 'no'. *'Benares mein curfew lag sakta hai, magar yahaan shaanti rehti hai'*—Benares might be under curfew, but here in Mughal Sarai there is always peace.

He went on, 'Look at me, for example. I live in a Hindu-dominated area, but I have never ever felt threatened.' My eyebrows went up involuntarily: all along I had presumed he was a Hindu—not that it mattered—because his name was Babu. He was quick to read my thoughts. 'Babu is my nickname, my full name is Muslimeen Ahmed,' he said rather apologetically, as if he was sorry that I had found out he was a Muslim.

Babu took leave, saying his family was waiting. My attention wandered to the other tables. On the one adjacent to mine sat two men who had just been served chilli chicken. They eyed the steaming dish with delight and turned around the chicken pieces with forks so that they cooled down a bit and did not burn their mouths.

Suddenly, a man on the table in front of theirs turned around and asked them, '*Kaisa hota hai yahaan ka chicken?*'— How does the chicken taste in this place? Even before any of the two could answer, he had already dug a fork into a piece and put it into his mouth.

His companion, however, was embarrassed. He said, '*Kahiye to hum bhi mangwaa lete hain*'—We can also order it if you like.

The shameless man, still chewing on the chicken, replied, '*Nahin, nahin, hum to bus dekh rahe thhe yahaan ka chicken kaisa hota hai*'—No, no, don't bother. I was just checking how good the chicken is.

Suddenly there was silence in the bar. Clearly, others had also noticed the man turning around and plunging a fork into the chicken ordered by total strangers. They all waited to see how the owners of the chilli chicken would react. Since the two men pretended as if nothing happened, the bar returned to its noisy self.

I somehow couldn't take my eyes off the shameless man. After he and his companion had finished their drinks and were about to leave, he once again turned around and plunged the fork into another piece of chicken. With the chicken still in his mouth, he motioned to his companion that they should get going.

The bar, which had once again collectively held its breath, resounded with laughter the moment the two men were out of sight.

The young Sikh was in splits. '*Yeh kya kar diya!*' he

teased the men who had just lost two precious chicken pieces to a rank stranger—How could you let this happen!

One of them replied sheepishly, *'Kya karen? Agar koi kaanta gaarhh they, kaise rok sakte hain?'*—What could we do? If someone decides to dig a fork, how could we stop him?

The Sikh was laughing uncontrollably. *'Ek baar garhhwaa diya to dobara gaarhhna hi thha'*—Since you let him dig once, he was bound to dig again.

There was another wave of laughter. The victim here was Indian hospitality. The shameless man, knowing that the two patrons would not outrightly object to him tasting their chicken, had not even waited for their permission. What he had committed was daylight robbery: gobbling up two of the eight pieces of chicken in a plate that had been ordered by total strangers with their hard-earned money.

I felt like having another drink. The idea was to linger on in the bar so that I could fill up my notebook with such anecdotes. Filling up the notebook was an excuse actually: my spirits were now high enough to make me want another drink and socialise with the people around me.

In states like Uttar Pradesh and Madhya Pradesh, alcohol is also packaged in 90 ml bottles called the *bachcha*, or child, which comes to your rescue when you are struck by the I-am-still-one-drink-short syndrome. It also comes handy in places where carrying bigger bottles can cause embarrassment or attract admonishment, such as trains. I sent the boy to get me a 'child' bottle of whisky.

By now the cash counter was occupied, by a tall, dark and well-built man. The black leather jacket he wore made him look even more intimidating. The way he ordered the boys around, I knew he ran the place. He barked some instructions, made some calculations on a piece of paper and then joined the Sikh and his companions on their table. It was clear that they were all friends, and that they gathered here almost every evening to spend the last few hours of an uneventful day.

After downing the *bachcha*, I could not resist joining them at their table. I was hoping the word 'journalist' would work here, and it did. The tall, dark man in leather jacket was indeed the owner of the bar. His name was Ramesh Gupta, and his family owned several shops in the town. The Sikh was a businessman who was born in Mughal Sarai. Two of the other men were preparing for the civil services exams and at the same time took coaching classes to prepare the younger generation of students for various entrance tests. Another was a booking clerk with the railways.

Indian hospitality took over. They asked me where I was staying. When I told them I was staying at Devi Lodge, they cried, almost in unison: '*Arre, aap wahaan kyon chale gaye?*'—What made you go there?

When I asked them what was wrong with the lodge, they said it was often raided by the police because people took call girls there. I wondered if that was the reason why the man at the lodge had been reluctant to have a chat with me.

They asked me about the tariff. When I told them, they almost jumped in disbelief. 'One hundred and eighty rupees? What are you saying! Only the other day I saw their pamphlet. They were letting out rooms for ninety rupees!' Ramesh, the owner of the bar, thundered.

Suddenly, plans were being made to rescue me from the lodge. The railway clerk said, 'Why don't you stay in a retiring room? There is something grand about the railways. As a journalist, you must come and experience the grandeur for yourself.'

I promised him I would, and we exchanged phone numbers so that he could call me and let me know if there was a room vacant at the station. He said he was going to the station right away—he was on night duty—and that he would call me within an hour.

'Don't worry,' Ramesh assured me, 'in case you don't find a room at the station, I will put you up in a hotel. But you must get out of that lodge tonight itself.' The others at the table agreed.

The clerk and the jolly Sikh left. I was left behind with the bar owner and the two aspirants for civil services. I asked them if they would like to have a drink on me. They didn't say yes, but they didn't say no either. I sent the boy for more whisky. Not wanting to be outdone in generosity, Ramesh called his cook and instructed him to prepare some chilli chicken without adding artificial colour.

'Don't add colour, *samjhey*?' he repeated several times, in case the cook added a pinch of the colouring agent out of habit.

Till then, I had no idea that artificial colour was being added to the dishes to spice up their looks. I couldn't make up my mind whether to feel honoured or cheated. I decided on feeling honoured because when you set out on such journeys, you take it for granted that the world is out to cheat you.

When the whisky and the chicken arrived, I asked

Ramesh to tell me about his bar: what kind of people usually came to drink?

'Ninety per cent of them are from the low class. Of them, sixty percent come here only to drink. Only five per cent come here for the food,' he said, and turned to the 'coaching' teachers for their approval—'*Kyon bhai, theek kahaa na* (Am I not right)?'

The two nodded in agreement.

'But there is one thing common among all those who come here,' he said, waving his index finger.

'What is it?' I asked. He was expecting me to ask that.

Ramesh replied: '*Yeh sab aayenge Ram ki tarah, aur jayenge Raavan ki tarah*'—When they walk in, they are as sober as Lord Rama, but when they leave, they behave like the [demon king] Ravana.

I asked him about Mughal Sarai. Did the town have any *sarai*, on inn, dating back to the Mughal period?

'*Koi sarai warai nahin hai* (there is no inn or whatever). When Mughal emperors travelled during those days, they easily found things for recreation in this place. *Yahaan unko randiyaan mil jaati theen* (they would find prostitutes here). That is why this place is called Mughal Sarai,' Ramesh explained.

His explanation did not go down well with the 'coaching class' teachers. '*Kaun class tak padhe ho bey?*' one of them asked Ramesh in irritation—Till which standard did you study, you idiot?

'*Kyon? B.Com tak padhe hain!*' Ramesh barked back— Why! I've done my B. Com.

The teacher replied, 'No wonder you don't know anything about history. The Mughals camped here because they found the place strategically convenient, not because of any *randi-wandi* (prostitutes and the like).'

I asked the teacher if he could tell me why exactly the town was called Mughal Sarai. He said he was not very sure, but it was possible that it acquired the name after Aurangzeb's army camped here before attacking Kashi (Benares). 'But I am not very sure,' he repeated. He promised to take me, the next morning, to some elders in the town who would know better.

The conversation then drifted to mundane things. Ramesh told me the next time I came to Mughal Sarai, I should bring my family along and stay with him. The gesture was alcohol-induced and therefore genuine, at least for the moment. I made a reciprocal gesture. Soon imaginary trips were being planned to Pondicherry and Bangalore, places close to Madras.

I was tipsy by now, but sober enough to remember that the railway clerk—who had promised to call me within an hour to let me know if there was a retiring room vacant at the station—had still not called. So I called him, but his phone was switched off.

'Don't worry,' Ramesh said, 'I will find you a hotel.'

It was 11 pm and Mughal Sarai was once again asleep. Ramesh's Bullet motorcycle, with me on the pillion, broke the silence of the night as we headed back to Devi Lodge to collect my belongings. He evidently took great care of the bike as if it were his child, and when I told him that he deserved to be featured in the local papers for owning it, his eyes filled with pride.

The man who ran the lodge was missing from the reception when we got in. Instead, a boy was loitering there. Ramesh, who was walking ahead of me in his enthusiasm to liberate me from the lodge, suddenly stopped like a cat that had run into a dog.

'*Arrey, yeh to Vijay ki gaadi hai! Woh yahaan kya kar raha hai*? (This is Vijay's bike! What on earth is he doing here?),' he exclaimed in surprise, pointing to a motorcycle parked in the compound of the lodge. Vijay was the railway clerk who had promised to get me a retiring room at the station.

After expressing his surprise, Ramesh suddenly went silent and followed me as I climbed up the stairs to collect my bags. My mind was busy putting two and two together: only a couple of hours before, these people were warning me against the call-girl business going on in the lodge, and now the clerk's bike was parked here and his mobile phone switched off. What should I make of it?

As I packed my bags, putting in the T-shirt and *lungi* I had planned to leave behind (I found that I did not have the heart to do so), Ramesh went to the bathroom and emptied his bladder while keeping the door wide open.

'*Waise kamraa bura nahin hai* (the room is not so bad),' he remarked as he came out of the bathroom, struggling with his trouser zip.

When we walked down to the reception, I saw the boy still loitering around. When I told him I was checking out, he ran out and returned, within a matter of seconds, to hand me twenty rupees. I suddenly remembered that I had paid an advance of Rs 200, while the tariff was Rs 180. I felt a little bad about leaving.

The hotel that Ramesh brought me to was right opposite the station. He knew the manager, a young man, who shook my hand effusively and offered me a discount. The stay was going to cost me only Rs 110 per night. I felt grateful.

This was the same hotel I had been turned away from the same morning, and right now, I was enjoying the best hospitality it could offer. The room boy (actually a middle-aged man who must have seen some forty winters in the same hotel) brought me bread and omelette. He also brought a fresh blanket. I slept well that night.

THE NEXT MORNING, I called the 'coaching class' teacher who had promised to take me to some of the old-time residents of Mughal Sarai. A woman answered the call, and she told me he was still sleeping. I called after an hour, and she told me he had stepped out and would be back any moment.

I called after twenty minutes, but the phone was switched off. My fault. As a connoisseur of alcohol, I should have known that promises made at a bar table, no matter how genuine while being made, are not to be taken seriously. I went down to take a walk along the road. After a good night's sleep, I expected to be more receptive to the town.

But the sun was rather harsh for a November morning. The heat, the general chaos in front of the station, the hangover from last night's drinking—they made me feel dizzy. I stood at the gate of the hotel for a while, trying to figure how, or where, I should begin.

My eyes fell on a small shop across the road, from whose signboard I gathered it sold sports goods for children. I went over and asked for a skipping rope—the idea was also to sweat out the alcohol I had imbibed. The rope the shopkeeper showed me seemed too short, but he insisted that its length was just right for me.

'Take my word. If it falls short, you can return it,' the shopkeeper assured. The old-world assurance, as against the take-it-or-leave-it attitude of present-day shopkeepers of his kind, made him endearing. With his unkempt grey beard and shabby clothes, he looked more like a sincere gardener employed in a British-era bungalow.

'How much,' I asked him.

'Ten rupees,' he replied from behind his missing teeth.

I gave him the money and asked him for his story. His name was Chhote Lal. He was sixty-eight years old. He father used to be employed in the *khaan-paan vibhaag*—pantry department—of the railways. Food in those days, he said, would be cooked only in pure ghee. He remembers his father telling stories about traders bringing in their merchandise in bullock carts and camel carts and camping by the Grand Trunk Road. When he was young, Mughal Sarai used to be a very small place, like a village, but now it had grown beyond recognition. The growth, he said, was because of the railways.

I asked him if the communal strife in Benares ever spilled over to his town—the question I had asked Babu, the marble man, the night before at the bar. Chhote Lal shook his head. 'These things happen in Benares, but never here,' he affirmed. 'I lived with Muslims in Kasai Mohal (butchers' colony) for a long time, but nothing ever happened.'

Suddenly realising that I was taking notes, he stopped. He asked me if he would get into any trouble with the police if I published whatever he had just said. I assured him my book had nothing to do with him, and pressed for more information about the town.

He paused for a while and said there was nothing much he could think of, except that Lal Bahadur Shastri was born here. I knew that. Then he said something which I didn't know: Jana Sangh ideologue Deen Dayal Upadhyay, who is revered by the Bharatiya Janata Party just as Mahatma Gandhi is revered by the Congress party, was found murdered in the railway yard of Mughal Sarai on the night of 11 February 1968.

His murder, till date, remains a mystery. I asked for details. Chhote Lal said he vaguely remembered the excitement in the town that had followed the discovery of the body, but nothing more.

'But, wait a minute, come with me,' he said, gesturing me to follow him. He left me at a neighbouring stationery shop, run by a forty-something man who had no time for me because the shop was bustling with customers.

I tried playing the 'journalist' card, but that didn't cut any ice because he himself was a journalist of sorts, stringing for a respectable Hindi daily. Anyhow, he answered my questions. Deen Dayal Upadhyay, he said, was indeed found murdered in Mughal Sarai, and that it was a local Jana Sangh acitivist called Gurubaksh Kapahi who had been called by the railway police to identify his body.

'Is Mr Kapahi still alive?'

'Yes.'

'Where can I find him?'

'He lives behind the police station, farther down the road. You can ask anybody for directions. He used to have a shop, Adarsh Vastu Bhandar, which is also a little farther down the road. But I think the shop has closed down,' the shopkeeper-cum-journalist replied, barely taking his eyes off the receipt book he was busy scribbling on.

I felt awkward to pester him with questions, but I had one more to ask: why was Mughal Sarai called Mughal Sarai?

'In the sixteenth century, when Humayun's army was on its way to Sasaram (in present-day Bihar) to fight Sher Shah Suri, it had camped here. That is how it got its name. Anything else you want to know? If you want to know more, ask them,' he said, pointing to a group of men standing in a small circle outside his shop.

All of them turned out to be journalists, stringing for some Hindi newspaper or the other, except for one man who claimed to be heading the local unit of a political party. The stationery shop seemed to be their meeting place, where they exchanged notes, news and gossip. They were very warm to me.

Mughal Sarai, they were unanimous, was a notorious place. The railway station, according to them, was the fountainhead of all evils. Pickpockets roamed the place. Ticket examiners were into extortion, preying on poor and voiceless passengers. Vendors were hand in glove with the railway officers. Policemen were hand in glove with the pickpockets.

'There is an old saying,' one of the journalists said, '*Sau chaayeen, ek Mughal Sarai*'—A hundred thefts add up to a Mughal Sarai.

Another chipped in: 'The ticket examiners, between themselves, make lakhs of rupees during festivals, when the trains run jam-packed. And they have been posted in

Mughal Sarai for the past twenty or twenty-five years. Nobody ever gets transferred. So you can imagine the power they wield here. Most *goondas* in Mughal Sarai are patronised by them.'

I asked them about Gurubaksh Kapahi, the man who had been called upon to identify Deen Dayal Upadhayay's body. They told me I would have to go to Adarsh Vastu Bhandar, a little farther down the road.

But hasn't that shut down?

No, they replied. One of the men said he had spotted Mr Kapahi at the shop only the other day.

I asked them about Lal Bahadur Shastri. They said he was born in the Kurkhala Central Colony, a railway settlement, in the house of his maternal grandfather, who taught at the local school—Railway Inter College. Shastri had studied in that school.

The colony, they said, was still there, but the old houses were gone. The school, however, was very much around.

I took their leave and strolled towards the station. On the walls of its compound I noticed handwritten slogans, '*Netaji jeevit hain, waapas aayenge neta ke roop mein*'—Netaji (Subhas Chandra Bose) is still alive, he will return as a leader.

I hailed a cycle-rickshaw. Adarsh Vastu Bhandar, as I had expected, turned out to be a grocery store, with huge jars of pickle adorning its frontage. The boys who held court in the absence of the owner—the chair at the cash counter was vacant—told me that Mr Kapahi rarely showed up these days and that it was his son who now ran the shop. The son, however, had gone home for lunch.

I asked if could have their mobile numbers. The attendants refused to oblige me, but they parted with a landline number. I called the number immediately, only to be told that Mr Kapahi had gone to attend a funeral and would only be back in the evening.

Would he be coming to the shop in the evening?

'No idea,' the man who answered the phone said.

I decided to walk back to the hotel. On the way, I stopped at the same stationery shop and bought a copy of *Cosmopolitan*, a magazine I would normally not spend money on but wouldn't mind flipping through at the dentist's clinic. The cover picture of a nattily dressed Arjun Rampal and the clever captions that promised you twenty-five ways of having great sex and thirty-five ways of looking good made the glossy stick out like a sore thumb on the display shelf. The sight of the magazine—and its incongruity with the setting of Mughal Sarai—made me feel at home. I was suddenly missing the big city.

In the hotel I ordered a lunch of steamed rice and *alu matar*. When the waiter came with the food, I presented him with the skipping rope I had bought from Chhote Lal's shop: it was indeed too short for me. The waiter was clearly overcome by gratitude because he quickly returned with slices of lemon and onions.

Food, for some unexplainable reason, is simple and delicious in the small hotels that dot the length of the River Ganges—or the Ganga. Hardly any culinary intricacy is involved in the cooking of *alu puri* or *alu matar*, yet you want to go back to them over and over again. The craving they induce is far stronger than the urge to savour a meat dish that has been painstakingly prepared for hours.

But then, I am speaking for myself—a reluctant non-vegetarian.

Over lunch, *Cosmopolitan* told me about 'The Dudes Every Girl Must Date' and the 'Surprising Turn-Ons Men Don't Tell You About'. The biggest revelation, however, came from the Cosmo Staff Poll—an impromptu survey conducted on six members of the magazine's staff. The subject, naturally, was men. The results of the survey:

> *A guy with a fabulous body or a fabulous sense of humour?*
> Body 0/Humour 6.
> *A regular but very well-dressed guy or a witty slob?*
> Well-dressed 3/Slob 3.
> *Rich as hell or sexy as hell?*
> Rich 4/Sexy 2.
> *A man great at oral sex or one who is well-endowed?*
> Oral 6/Size 0.
> *Very hairy chest versus a waxed chest?*
> Hair 6/Wax 0.

Lunch over, my mind returned to Gurubaksh Kapahi. How do I find this man? I called his home again, only to be told that he still hadn't returned from the funeral. I was asked to call at eight in the evening. I returned to the *Cosmopolitan*. I had one more day to track him down.

SHORTLY BEFORE SUNSET, I hailed a cycle-rickshaw for the Railway Inter College, the school where India's most humble prime minister had studied.

Branching off the Grand Trunk Road—or GT Road,

as it is famously called—we passed, at leisurely pace, the sprawling offices of the railways and the quarters of their employees. The chirping of homeward-bound birds and the shouts of children playing cricket came as a relief from the chaos on the GT Road that my ears were now getting used to.

The road soon snaked into a vast expanse where, on the horizon, the orange sky stooped to meet the earth. Every now and then, the wheels of the rickshaw would go over abandoned rail tracks—a reminder that this was a railway town.

Finally, we pedalled into a railway settlement and soon I was standing outside a red-brick building in whose compound stood a fighter aircraft of the Indian Air Force. This was the Railway Inter College. The gate was locked. A few boys were loitering around. I went over to one of them and asked if there was a watchman who could open the gate for me.

'Don't worry about the lock,' he said, 'just follow me'.

He climbed over the gate and jumped to the other side, and helped me do the same. Immediately, the other boys followed suit. Nearly a dozen boys peered over my shoulder as I scribbled, in fading light, the writing on the plaque that explained the presence of the aircraft:

Dedicated to GURUS of Eastern Railway Intermediate
College, Mughal Sarai
By Ex-Student Air Marshal K. S. Chaturvedi, VSM
AOC-in-C, Maintenance Command, IAF
Son of Late Shiva Kumar Chaturvedi and
Smt Laxmi Chaturvedi
10 November 2006.

It was the case of a grateful student giving something back to his alma mater. I wondered if Lal Bahadur Shastri had given anything back to the school after he became the prime minister. In fact, I found no visible signs of Shastri having studied there, though from the boys I learned there was a plaque in one of the classrooms acknowledging his association with the school. But the building was locked—even the boys could not help me get in.

I shook their hands and sat on the rickshaw. I asked them for directions to Kurkhala Central Colony, where Shastri had been born 104 years ago. They said it was not very far, and that Phalaahaari Baba—the saint who lives on fruits—should be able to provide me details about the former prime minister's birthplace. The Baba, they said, lived in a Hanuman temple in the colony.

It was pleasantly chilly now, and as we pedalled from one railway settlement to another, my mind kept going back to Ramesh Gupta's bar. I felt I was missing all the action there. I decided to return there for a drink after I had met Phalaahaari Baba. I badly needed one after the back-breaking rickshaw ride.

At the Hanuman temple, which stood right in the middle of the colony that was now settling into the silence of the night, a group of women sat before the deity and sang *bhajans*. One of them played the *dholak* and another clanged the cymbals. I tiptoed past them, and went into a crudely constructed building in the compound and asked for the Baba.

'Yes *babu*, I am Phalaahaari Baba.'

He was a tall man, rather well built, and his face shone as if he had donned a mild coat of greasepaint to take part in a TV show. He must have been around sixty. He showed me into a large but very modestly furnished room that had pictures of Hanuman and other gods placed against one wall. In one corner, on the floor, sat an electric heater and next to it a plate with a pile of freshly-chopped vegetables.

'That's my dinner,' he said when he caught me looking at the vegetables. 'I boil them myself.'

The Baba spread a blanket on the floor, and as we sat down, he sent for tea.

'*Haan babu, boliye kya jaanna chaahte hain?*' he asked—Yes sir, what would you like to know?

Everything, I told him.

He fixed his gaze at the floor for a few moments, and then started talking.

Phalaahaari Baba, who was born in 1927 in Baluaghat in eastern Uttar Pradesh, has been in this temple for twenty-eight years now. Before that, he had been a constable with the Railway Protection Force, for twenty-two years. His life was as uneventful as that of any other beat constable, but his posting in Calcutta had proved to be a turning point. One day, while he was on duty on a train, the electrical wiring got stolen from a compartment. The blame for the theft fell on Phalaahaari Baba. He was served with a notice and had an enquiry set up against him. Once he left the job, he sought the permission of his wife and children to leave home. He wandered around for a while in search of God before settling at the temple, which was then looked after by a Naga sadhu. He helped the Naga sadhu, who was a heart patient, repair the temple, and when the sadhu died, he took charge of the temple. He has been here ever since, looking after the small temple and counselling people in the neighbourhood when they come to him with their troubles. He ventures out only occasionally, making trips to places like Brindavan or Gangotri.

I asked him his name. He refused to tell me: 'It no longer matters, *babu*. Now they call me Phalaahaari Baba. That name should suffice.'

I asked him about the theft: did he steal the wires, or was he blamed for no fault of his? Once again, he tickled my curiosity rather than satisfying it: '*Ab jaane dijiye babu, kuchh hamaari bhi galti thi*'—Let bygones be bygones, I must have also been at fault.

I asked him if he had left the job on his own or had been asked to leave. He again dismissed my question politely: 'It no longer matters, *babu*. It's an old story.'

The tea arrived, and along with it an orange and a banana which were meant for me. Suddenly, I envied this man. He was actually eighty, but looked barely sixty. And unlike me and billions of others, he did not carry the burden of proving anything to anyone. He was what he was—a simple man, who claimed no special powers when he easily could have, living in the midst of people whose faith in religion can make them completely blind to reason. But he was content tending to this small temple and professing his love for Lord Hanuman and playing the elderly uncle to the residents of the colony.

Even the simplest of lives must have a routine. Or maybe, it is the routine that makes lives simple. Phalaahaari Baba rises at three every morning and, after his ablutions, chants prayers till sunrise, when it is time for breathing exercises and meditation. At seven o' clock, he conducts an *aarti*—the ritual waving of lights—at the temple. This is followed by tea. At noon, he has a brunch of fruits and boiled vegetables. At nine in the evening, he leads another *aarti*, which is followed by dinner that comprises, once again, boiled vegetables.

'I hardly fall ill. I always feel light,' he said when I asked him about the benefits of subsisting on fruits and boiled vegetables.

I looked at my watch. It was 8.30. It would soon be time for his evening *aarti*. Also, the vegetables were waiting to be boiled. I bowed before him and took leave. The women were still singing in chorus. Outside, the rickshaw-puller was still waiting for me.

On the way back to the hotel, I noticed, on a railway overbridge, posters of another Bhojpuri film, *Rangbaaz Aashiq*—loosely translated, the Flamboyant Lover. 'Rangbaaz' was a term I had grown up with in Kanpur. It is an adjective hurled sarcastically at a show-off.

It suddenly struck me that I had not seen a single hoarding or a poster of a Hindi film in Mughal Sarai. I had been reading about the boom in the Bhojpuri film industry, but I had no idea that it had actually elbowed out Bollywood stars from this stretch of the Hindi heartland.

Once back on the GT Road, I couldn't resist trying my luck at Gurubaksh Kapahi's shop once again—in case he happened to be there. At last, he was there.

'Are you Mr Kapahi?' I asked the elderly man who was now seated at the cash counter, almost hidden by the jars of pickle.

He looked up and said, 'Yes, and you are?'

I introduced myself and told him that I wanted to know about the fateful morning when he had been called upon to identify the body of Deen Dayal Upadhayay.

'I think you want to see my father.'

'That's right. But he has been out all day.'

'He must be home by now,' said the younger Kapahi, looking at his watch.

'Does he carry a mobile phone?'

'Don't worry. He must be home by now. You can talk to him there.'

The rickshaw-puller, once again, took me into a maze of lanes. It wasn't difficult finding Mr Kapahi's house as almost everybody seemed to know him and gave us directions as we went from one lane to another.

At Mr Kapahi's house, there was no bell, so I knocked at the door that was ajar and exposed a corridor. No response. I knocked harder, still no response. At the laundry shop on the street corner, which was the landmark that had been given to me, a boy told me that he had seen Mr Kapahi walk out of his house only a few minutes ago.

'But I thought he was just back from a funeral,' I said.

'I don't know about that. But I just saw him going this way,' the boy said, pointing to the GT Road.

I went back to Adarsh Vastu Bhandar, to report to the younger Kapahi that his father was not to be found at home. He—finally—gave me his father's mobile number and asked me to call.

Mr Gurubaksh Kapahi, it turned out, was now attending a wedding, after having attended a funeral. The wedding hall was farther up the road, closer to my hotel.

'Could I come over?' I asked Mr Gurubaksh Kapahi.

'Of course, most welcome,' he said, as if he were the bride's father.

The rickshaw-puller, who had been overhearing my part of the conversation, knew where to take me and climbed up his seat as soon as I hung up. Within minutes, I was climbing the steps of a wedding hall where half-a-dozen male members of the bride's family waited eagerly for the groom's party to arrive.

I was received warmly by a suit-clad elderly man, perhaps the father of the bride, and when I asked for Mr Kapahi, he took me to yet another elderly man wearing a white kurta-pyjama.

'So you are the one who has been looking for me!' Mr Kapahi smiled.

He was obviously a respected figure in Mughal Sarai. Most of the invitees who trooped in for the wedding acknowledged his presence by either touching his feet or bowing to him with folded hands. Mr Kapahi returned their greetings with a boyish grin. He motioned me to a chair next to him and put his arm around me: 'So tell me, what is it that you want to know?'

12 FEBRUARY 1968: Gurubaksh Kapahi, an active member of the Rashtriya Swayamsewak Sangh, or the RSS—the fountainhead of the Jana Sangh, which later became the Bharatiya Janata Party—had just finished his bath and was engrossed in his daily meditation when, around 8.30 a.m., a constable of the Railway Protection Force came knocking.

'The constable told me, "There's a body lying at the station. I would like you to come with me and identify it." Entire Mughal Sarai knew I was a Jana Sangh worker,' said Mr Kapahi.

At the station, Mr Kapahi had instantly recognised Deen Dayal Upadhyay whose body, he said, was lying on the floor, tied-up like an unclaimed corpse, at the door of the railway police station.

'I kept telling them, "Look, this is Panditji. You can't keep him on the floor like this." By then, some other swayamsewaks had arrived, and only when we made a noise did they remove the body from the floor,' he said.

Even as Mr Kapahi was recalling one of the most important moments of his life, the elderly man who had welcomed me into the hall came to ask if I would like to eat something. He and the other male members of the family were now getting restless. The groom's party—the *baraat*—was taking way too long to arrive. I politely refused: I was only a gate-crasher.

Mr Kapahi went on, 'We made a call to Jaunpur, where Guruji (Guru Golwalker, then the RSS head) was attending a function. We then took the body to Benares Civil Lines. People started coming in. Balraj Madhok and Atal Behari Vajpayee flew down. Then Guruji came. He looked at Deen Dayalji and said, "How could this happen to you?" Guruji never kept well after that. Bhausaheb Deoras (who was to succeed Golwalkar as the RSS chief) also arrived. Finally a government plane was sent to take the body to Delhi.'

Mr Kapahi remembers the slogans from his Jana Sangh days by heart: *Hamara naara akhand Bharat* (Our slogan, unified India); *Kashmir hamara hai* (Kashmir is ours); *Jitna Nehru garjega, utna Jana Sangh barsega* (the more Nehru thunders, the more heavily Jana Sangh will come down on him). He and thousands of other Jana Sanghis had raised these slogans at Ajmeri Gate in Delhi in 1953, when the party, led by Syama Prasad Mookerjee, was agitating against the special status being granted to Kashmir under the Constitution.

Mr Kapahi's career as a political worker has not gone unacknowledged. Today, he leads the peaceful life of a Loktantra Senani—soldier of democracy—entitled to a monthly pension of Rs 2,500 and a free bus pass. It is a different matter that the Loktantra Senani scheme was initiated by RSS-baiter Mulayam Singh Yadav, during his latest stint as the chief minister of Uttar Pradesh.

Outside the wedding hall, the rickshaw-puller was waiting for me. I told him to drop me at the hotel. On the way, I passed Ramesh Gupta's bar. Until a couple of hours ago, I was itching to go there, but right now I did not feel like it. Perhaps it was the effect of meeting Phalaahari Baba.

At the hotel gate, as I reached for my wallet, I wanted to ask the rickshaw-puller how much I should pay him but I did not. After pedalling me around the whole evening, it would be mentally taxing for him to arrive at a figure. So I handed him a hundred-rupee note. At first he was shocked, but he quickly recovered from the shock and kissed the note and then touched it to his forehead and chest and put it in his pocket.

FAITH AND CURIOSITY are two things that usually bring people to Benares. I was now headed there partly for both. Even though I'm not a staunch believer in god, I am a great fan of Shiva, the Lord of Destruction, whose presence looms large over Benares. And even though I'd been to Benares before, I wasn't old—and wise—enough back then to grasp the nuances that make the city a magnet to mankind. And since I was almost done with Mughal Sarai, and had an entire day to myself, why not?

I set out on an aged Ambassador that was bereft of its rear-view mirrors and driven by a boy called Ram Ratan, whose age, as I learned only after reaching Benares, was only seventeen years. He had his palm pressed to the horn throughout, as if he had to urgently answer nature's call upon reaching Benares. As a result I barely enjoyed the drive: I kept wondering if I would make it in one piece. Not that there was much to enjoy except flat lands on either side of the road on which ugly buildings sprouted.

Just as we neared Benares, I found the car trailing a jeep that was packed with people and on the roof of which a body on a bier was securely tied up. The shroud was colourful and shiny: an indication that it could be the body of a *suhaagan*—a woman whose husband was still alive and therefore escaped the misfortune of being widowed. Ram Ratan, somehow, didn't have the heart to overtake the jeep. He kept slow, and soon we reached a bridge from where the sight that has sold millions of picture postcards unfolded: the ghats of Benares dotted with mushroom-like canopies.

Old Benares is a maze of streets along the river—some streets so narrow that you can block them by stretching out your arms. Tucked away in one such street is the Vishwanath temple. I wanted to go there the first thing. After all, I owed my name to it: my maternal grandfather happened to be visiting the temple a few days before or after I was born, and he had decided to name me after the god.

My being a fan of Shiva, though, has nothing to do with my name, which I hate at times because I find it too long and old-fashioned. I love Shiva because he is the coolest god that can be: happy-go-lucky, kind, wild, who drank, who danced, who smoked and who founded yoga. You don't have to be a staunch Hindu, or even a believer for that matter, to be able to connect with him.

But the Vishwanath temple, at least the way it is now, can be a disappointment for a Shiva fan. After the blasts at the Sankat Mochan temple in March 2006, the security is extremely and understandably tight. (A day after my visit, bombs went off at the local court, killing nine people.)

These days, most of the shops that sell offerings also have lockers where you are required to deposit your belongings before entering the temple. It goes without saying that you can use the locker facility only if you purchase the offerings from that shop. I bought flowers and sweets for Rs 51, and in return, was allowed to use a locker in which I placed my two mobile phones and a Mont Blanc fountain pen. With my lifelines locked up in the shop of a flower seller, my mind wasn't entirely at peace during my appointment with the Lord.

After being frisked at the entrance, I joined the queue of other devotees. 'Cover the basket with your hands,' a security guard told me. But there was so much of pushing around that I did not pay attention to him.

Pandas—the bandits who promise you the attention of God—kept coming. I told them I was not only a local but also a journalist who was capable of finding his way in.

To which they said: 'If people like you ignore us, sir, how will we survive?' I ignored them. I did not want them to survive.

The legendary stories about their money-extracting skills would make a thief want to change his profession. The driver later told me over lunch how one rich pilgrim was recently persuaded to shell out a lakh of rupees in the name of Lord Vishwanath. The pilgrim, realising his folly, had reported the matter to the police. By then, the panda who had pocketed the sum had disappeared, never to be seen in Benares again. It escaped me how anyone in his right mind could venture into a temple such as this with so much of money.

Before being let into the sanctum sanctorum, the devotees were frisked once again and their baskets put through metal detectors. As I stood in the queue, waiting for it to move forward, a baby monkey pounced on my basket, making away with the packet of sweets. I was too stunned to react for a while. As I went about collecting the scattered offerings from my basket, I realised why the guard had asked me to cover it with my hands. He knew monkeys better, just as the baby monkey knew that a man lost in thoughts was an easy target.

'No, you cannot use that garland. It has touched the ground,' someone told me. It was a priest who had suddenly appeared from nowhere. Apart from the few flowers and a packet of vermillion that remained in the basket, I had nothing to offer to Shiva. The fifty-one rupees had gone down the drain.

Inside the sanctorum, the priest who sat next to the historical lingam hardly paid any attention to the baskets people were carrying. He seemed to have been appointed to the post only to scold devotees: 'Don't touch this!' 'Don't do this!' 'Don't do that!' 'Enough now!' 'Keep moving!'

While I was still watching him thunder at a hapless group of pilgrims from Tamil Nadu, a woman constable showed me the door, literally and rather rudely, 'Enough, now move on.'

Outside the temple, Ram Ratan was waiting for me. I asked him to show me the ghats. 'Follow me,' he said.

In the maze of the narrow streets where the shops piqued my curiosity and where one had to navigate through a sea of pilgrims, it was impossible to keep pace with him. He would always race out of sight, and it would be a while before I could catch up with him, only to lose him all over again. His legs were showing the same impatience that his palm had with the car horn. But I couldn't have done without him now: he knew the streets better than the back of his palm.

The steps of the famous Dashashwamedha ghat were being washed with the help of hosepipes in preparation for a government-sponsored cultural festival that was to start in a couple of days. The river is considered to be a cleanser for mankind, but the steps leading to it must now be cleaned manually. I stood at the freshly-cleaned steps for a while and looked at the river. I called up my boss in Chennai.

'Guess where I am.'

'Where are you?' she asked.

'Take a guess.'

'Somewhere in Mughal Sarai, I guess.'

'I'm in Benares.'

'Benares!' she was genuinely surprised. 'What on earth are you doing there? When did you get there?'

Her surprise was understandable: Mughal Sarai, even though its name gives off a whiff of history, is unlikely to interest anyone unless you have routinely passed its railway station during childhood—a time when you read about the Mughal emperors and when names of places inspire larger-than-life images. But Benares, barely ten kilometres away, is another planet. Technically, I was standing by a colourless river in a small town in Uttar Pradesh, watching people go about their business. But the moment you identify the river and the town, the earth under your feet becomes worthy of worship. Unlike other places whose history is measured in years, Benares has defied time: its history is as enchanting as, and entwined with, that of the gods.

If only history had provided mankind with a TV screen and a rewind button to watch what was going on, at exactly the same spot you stood, on dates of your choice! I pretty much doubt if Benares would have looked any different had I scanned footages through the centuries.

But I would have certainly kept pressing the pause button to look out for certain characters: Goswami Tulsidas, who wrote the Ramayana for the layman; or Trailanga Swami, the pot-bellied naked saint who is said to have lived for three hundred years, most of which he spent in meditation either by floating in the river or sitting by its banks; or Allan Ginsberg, the Beat poet, who roamed the ghats in search of God. It is a different matter that I wouldn't have recognised any of them. The only person I recognised in Benares was Ram Ratan, and he was now waiting—impatiently as ever—for me.

We walked down the steps and he haggled with a boatman for a ride on the Ganga. The boatman asked for

Rs 40, but Ram Ratan brought the figure down to Rs 20. As we got onto the boat, I found a Western couple, flashing practised smiles, already seated on its bow, and I realised why the boatman had brought down the fare without much resistance. The couple would have paid him enough for him to survive without touching the oars for the rest of the week.

Soon I was in the middle of the river, and from here, under the afternoon winter sun, Benares was fully living up to its picture-postcard image: the sights were close enough to be savoured, and the sounds distant enough not to spoil the sights—all for Rs 20.

FOR LUNCH, RAM RATAN took me to a restaurant-cum-sweetshop that seemed to be one of the best in town. No sooner had we taken our seats—Ram Ratan was initially hesitant to share the table with me—than two plates of *rasagullas* arrived. I presumed they were complimentary and checked with Ram Ratan if they were indeed so. He nodded in agreement. While having the *rasagullas*, I scanned the menu. I asked him what he would like to have. 'Anything,' he replied with his trademark impatience.

I ordered two plates of *samosas*. I had not had them in ages. Over *samosas*, I made small talk with him—about Benares, about the pandas, about himself. I asked him how old he was.

'Seventeen,' he replied, then instantly changing his mind, 'Eighteen'. He had studied till class five and was always interested in 'drivery'—being a driver. So he began driving a weather-beaten Ambassador, loaned by an uncle.

Once the *samosas* got over, I felt like ordering *alu paratha*. But Ram Ratan was itching to get away. As a professional driver, he was perhaps more used to his clients sitting either behind him or next to him, but certainly not facing him. Our current position was clearly making him uncomfortable, and he excused himself.

'I need to meet a friend,' he said.

'Do you have friends here?' I asked.

'Yes, he has a shop here. I won't take long. In any case, my mobile phone is on. Give me a missed call.'

I ate my *paratha* alone, watching other customers who were now trooping in and being served with the complimentary *rasagulla*. Once I finished eating and asked for the bill, I found that I was paying for the *rasagullas* as well. It was too late and foolish to say, 'But I didn't ask for them.'

Perhaps serving the spongy sweet was a way of extracting a cover charge: in case people walked in and left after having a free glass of water, which is not unimaginable in a town where thousands of thirsty souls pour in every single day.

I summoned Ram Ratan and together we walked to the car which was parked at a distance. On the way, I lost count of the funeral processions that were coming in: some processions celebrated the deliverance of their dead with drum beats and dancing; the others glumly chanted, '*Ram naam satya hai.*'

It was like witnessing a carnival of the dead, with each procession showcasing its bier and the dead joyfully raising invisible thumbs from under their shrouds to exclaim, 'We made it! We made it to Benares!'

The images of the bedecked biers kept swimming in my head as the Ambassador rattled down the dusty road to Mughal Sarai. Everybody has to die one day, but you don't want to be reminded of that, do you? It is, however, not the thought of your own death that makes the sight of the biers so terrifying: it is actually the thought of your near and dear ones being carried away in that fashion. It is a thought you consider secretly in the deepest crevices of your heart, not even sharing it aloud with your own self.

MY LAST EVENING IN Mughal Sarai: I had a train to catch at two in the morning. Should I take a cycle-rickshaw and roam the town one last time, or spend some time in Ramesh Gupta's bar, from where one walks out feeling good? I decided to feel good in the hotel room itself and sent for a bottle of whisky.

Even as I drank, I wrote for a while and then read, and was into my third drink when I felt the need for a conversation. I called up Ramesh Gupta. He was very pleased to hear from me and said he would come soon. I began to sip my drink slowly, in order to be left with enough whisky to share by the time he arrived.

An hour passed. I started packing. There were too many things lying around which had to be put into the bag before alcohol could make me blind to them—phone chargers, notebook, pens, razor. My rucksack packed, I was now ready to leave—only that I had nowhere to go for another three hours. I switched on the small TV which I had ignored all this while. The news was bad: a curfew had been declared in Calcutta, where I would be reaching the next morning. The Army had been deployed in parts of the city after a group of Muslim youths led a violent protest demanding that the self-exiled Bangladeshi writer Taslima Nasreen be thrown out of India. Will the trains be allowed into Calcutta at all?

Ramesh Gupta barged in. He gave me a hug. 'Look, I made it!' he exclaimed and then handed me a small box of sweets. 'This is for you to have during the journey.'

I poured drinks for both of us and the room suddenly became lively. We began planning itineraries: the places to visit when he and his family came to Madras, and the places to see when I returned to Mughal Sarai with my family.

'The next time, you will have to stay with me,' he pointed his index finger menacingly at me, 'I will not take no for an answer.'

He also made me promise that I will bring my wife along the next time. I extracted a similar promise.

Alcohol was talking now. Ramesh began expounding on the theory of friendship. Friendship, he said, was possible only between equals.

'Take us, for example,' he said. 'You are a big journalist, correct? Now, I may not be highly educated, but I make up for that with my wealth. So that makes us equals, correct?'

'Correct,' I replied.

'Two people might be the best of friends, but they should also have self-respect, correct?' he asked. 'I don't know if you recall, but the other night when you made drinks for all of us, I was hesitant to touch it. Did you notice that or not?'

I had not, but I said I had.

'Had I grabbed the drink like a greedy man that night,' he explained, 'you would have lost all respect for me. Tomorrow, if I come to Chennai and if you see me reaching for my wallet, I know you will stop me by saying, "Ramesh *bhai*, you are in Chennai. You are my guest. I am not going to let you pay for anything." Correct? But had I pounced on the drink that night, you would treat me differently.'

Shortly after midnight Ramesh took leave. His said his wife was waiting. I was hoping that he would keep me company till I left for the station. After he left, I tried reading, but I found myself looking at the watch again and again, to see if it was time for the train. So I decided to kill the remaining time at the station rather than in the room, which now seemed depressing anyway.

While walking down to the reception, I made a mental calculation of the tariff: two days would cost me Rs 220, and minus the Rs 100 advance I had already paid, I owed them Rs 120.

'You total bill amount is Rs 330, sir,' the manager said with a smile.

'But I thought the rent was Rs 110?'

'Yes, sir. Rs 110 multiplied by three.'

'But I stayed only for two days.'

'True, sir, but we go by the twenty-four-hour cycle. Here, look at the register. That night you checked in at 12.05 am, and now it is 1.30 am You have exceeded forty-eight hours. So it becomes three days.'

'You could have reminded me. I was doing nothing upstairs. Moreover, I overstayed only by ninety minutes.'

'I know sir, but that is the rule.' He was no longer smiling. He was not even looking at me.

I paid up. An extra hundred rupees did not hurt, but the fact that he could be so unreasonable and inconsiderate did. As I walked across to the station, I decided to call Ramesh Gupta and lodge a protest. I just wanted to let him know. At first my call went unanswered, and then his phone was switched off.

THE DEPARTURE TIME ON the ticket was printed as 1.55 am, when the Howrah-bound Rajdhani Express, coming from Delhi, would leave Mughal Sarai after a five-minute halt. At the station, making my way through an assorted crowd of humans and animals, namely cows and dogs, I reached the enquiry office where, on a white board, the status of various incoming trains had been handwritten in Hindi. I noticed the word 'Gaya' against Rajdhani Express. My heart sank.

'Gaya', in Hindi, means gone.

Only after several anxious moments did it strike me that Gaya, in this case, was the station in Bihar where Rajdhani Express would be making a scheduled stop on its way to Howrah. But I could not entirely recover from the shock until I woke up the next morning to the railways breakfast of bread, butter and cutlet.

KAMA COUNTRY BECKONS
JHANSI

THERE ARE TWO THINGS you prepare yourself for while stepping out of a railway station in India, especially north India.

One is, of course, the horde of autorickshaw drivers and rickshaw-pullers who almost grab you by the arm in their eagerness to take you to your destination. The other is the clutter around it: cheap hotels, food stalls, *paan* shops, phone booths and dilapidated houses that must be standing from the time the station received its first train.

When the train brought me to Jhansi, I was free of many anxieties, unlike during my arrival in Mughal Sarai, because the sun was on my side. It was only five in the evening and only a matter of minutes before I would confidently stride out of the station and walk into one of the hotels surrounding it.

So I brushed aside the man who asked me the question I dreaded the most: '*Saahab, kahaan jaana hai?*'—Sir, where would you like to go? He was a 'tempo' driver—the 'tempo' being a three-wheeled taxi that can carry up to ten passengers.

But Jhansi station stood like an island at the intersection of three wide roads which led to I had no idea where.

I saw the 'tempo' driver approaching me again. He walked with deliberate steps, as if he was hiding a knife behind him. His eyes clearly said: 'I could easily tell you did not know a soul in this city. Now you are at my mercy.'

But his lips merely repeated his question, '*Saahab, kahaan jaana hai?*'

Nowhere, I told him, and started walking on the road that ran perpendicular to the station. It must lead somewhere. Having pretended like someone who knew the town like the back of his hand, I would look foolish surrendering to him.

Had I known where exactly I was headed, this walk would have been one of the most pleasant in my life. The breeze was pleasant and the road wide and tree-lined. The chirping of the birds was louder than the noise made by passing vehicles. What more could a traveller ask for?

This seemed to be an important road for I passed one government bungalow after another. They had lawns as big as football fields. Then appeared a playground, where a football match was on. The match, I am sure, was to find a mention in the next morning's papers because it was being witnessed by a row of distinguished-looking men who sat in isolation from the rest of the spectators. In all probability, they were either senior officers of the army, in their evening civvies, or the local bosses of the railways: Jhansi, synonymous with the Maratha warrior Laxmibai, houses a large cantonment and also a division of the railways.

A peanut-seller had parked his pushcart by the pavement and was watching the game. I bought peanuts for two rupees and asked him if I could find a hotel nearby. 'Keep going straight. You will find all the hotels there.'

'How far?' I asked.

'Not even a kilometre,' he replied. He was more eager to return to the football match, which must have been in its final moments now because the sun was beginning to set.

I walked past many more bungalows. A woman, who must have been in her early thirties and who wore trousers that emphasised her ample bottom, was herding her bicycle-riding child back home, into one of the bungalows.

I imagined walking up to her and introducing myself, in English. Fluency in English can work wonders in north Indian towns. It is the ultimate benchmark of sophistication, the logic being that if you can speak fluent English, you must have been to a 'convent' school, and if you have been to a 'convent' school, you must have had a decent education.

The logic, which is not entirely irrational, is so deep-rooted that even when you converse with people in chaste Hindi, and once they come to know that you belong to the English-speaking lot, they tend to reply with whatever phrases of English they have at their disposal. The idea is to tell you that they too know English. But this woman looked the kind who not only spoke English fluently but also made sure that it was the only language spoken at home—at least for the child's sake.

'Excuse me, ma'am, do you think I can find a hotel around?'

'Oh yes, there are quite a few down the road. Keep walking.'

'Thank you.'

'Wait a minute. You're walking all the way from the station, aren't you?'

'That's right.'

'Then why don't you come home and have some coffee? My husband will be happy to see a journalist. He'd be back any moment.'

'Why not?'

The imaginary conversation ended as soon she faded inside the gates of her bungalow. I kept walking. Before long, the road terminated at a traffic intersection and I found myself—to my great relief—in the middle of the chaos of a busy town. I had expected this chaos right outside the railway station, but never mind. The walk had been worth it.

I approached yet another peanut-seller. Winter is peanuts time in north India. Eating roasted peanuts, or *moong phali*, is a great pastime in itself, just like munching on popcorn at the movies. But there's a difference between popcorn and peanuts: you munch on popcorn only when you go to the movies, whereas when you start munching on peanuts, life itself becomes a movie and you become a passive spectator for that duration, addictively cracking open one shell after the other and putting the nuts into your mouth.

I asked the peanut-seller where I was.

'Elite Chauraha,' he replied—Elite intersection.

The intersection, I later learned, had borrowed its

name from a cinema hall that stands there and is the nucleus of Jhansi: the traffic island here regulates the movement of the entire town. In fact, the island is also the nucleus of India as far as the road map is concerned: vehicles headed from one corner of India to the other, be it Ahmedabad to Asansol or Kashmir to Kanyakumari, have to touch Elite intersection, where I stood now like a fresh graduate at the crossroads of his life, clueless about which path to pursue. The sun was still on my side.

'*Yahaan koi hotel-wotel milega?*' I asked the peanut-seller—Are there any hotels around here?

He had just begun to rattle off names of hotels when, to my great surprise, I heard my name being called from behind—clearly and loudly. I turned around, and it took me precisely two seconds to place the face I had last seen twenty years ago. My luck changed.

Vikas Saxena was my junior at school in Kanpur. I don't recall the two of us having even a single conversation during all those years at school: we only acknowledged each other's presence with a smile or a hello. That familiarity was now paying dividends after two decades as Vikas and I stood face to face like long-lost friends. We were now off on his scooter to what according to him was the best hotel in Jhansi.

Till a moment ago, I was a nervous witness to the chaos at the Elite intersection. Now I was gleefully a part of it.

The hotel was pleasant indeed. It had a lobby and a computerised reception desk manned by courteous staff. The receptionist himself showed me some of the rooms so that I could choose. I couldn't have asked for more.

Soon, Vikas and I were sitting in my air-conditioned

room, taking stock of the water that had flowed under the bridge all these years. Even though we hardly knew each other at school, we had plenty of friends in common—people I had lost track of but always wondered what they must be up to.

Vikas, with whatever information he had at his disposal, updated me about their lives. Some of them were doing very well, a few extraordinarily well: one of them was in NASA, another in the IAS, while a few others had taken the IIT-to-IIM route. A majority of them, however, had settled into the humdrum of middle-class life—working in banks or insurance companies or as sales managers with pharmaceutical companies. The ones who had joined the Army had now reached the rank of colonel.

Vikas said he too was doing very well until a few years ago, making a lot of money—seventy lakhs of rupees, according to him—from the stock exchange at Kanpur. But something went wrong and he lost all the money and he had moved to Jhansi at the insistence of his parents-in-law, who lived in the town. He explained to me what had gone wrong, but since I have no understanding of the mechanics of the stock market, I couldn't grasp the nuances of his story.

But he wasn't too badly off in Jhansi, where he supplied surgical instruments to local hospitals, including the ones run by the railways. 'I had to start from scratch. Over the years I managed to generate credibility and began to get business,' he said.

Listening to him, I did not realise that he had switched the TV on and was watching NDTV Profit channel even as he was talking to me. It happened to be a day when the Sensex had undergone a rollercoaster ride, changing the course of the evening for millions of people, and it must have been quite a task for Vikas to divide his attention between me and the excited anchors of the news channel.

I asked him about Jhansi. '*Chhota sa shahar hai. Kya rakkha hai yahaan,*' he dismissed the question—It is a small town, there's nothing out here.

His attention returned to the TV. He was watching the news about the rise and fall of the Sensex, just like a retired cricketer would be watching a one-day match: been there and done that, but still catching up with what's going on.

My mind was on Jhansi. I mentally planned an itinerary for the next two days, even though I was clueless about what all there was to see in the town. But I was sure I would find something. At least there was the fort from where Laxmibai, the queen of Jhansi, had taken the plunge on horseback, with her adopted son Damodar strapped to her back. She had died fighting the British and become a symbol of patriotism and female valour. Until not very long ago, almost every schoolgirl aspired to be as brave as the Rani of Jhansi.

Vikas asked me what my plans were for the evening. I said I had no plans yet. 'In that case,' he said, 'I will come back in a while. We can go out for a drink. From there we can go home for dinner.'

I asked him about the places I must visit. As I had expected, he said there was nothing much to see in Jhansi except the fort. But there was Orchha, 19 km away, and Khajuraho, 176 km away. I decided to pack these places into my itinerary. How could one miss going to Khajuraho after having come all the way to Jhansi which, as I discovered, was the nearest convenient railhead?

The only time I had been to Khajuraho was in 1978, as an eight-year-old, when one was still several years away from discovering the sensations that its temples celebrated. It had been a picnic. At four in the morning one Sunday, about two dozen Bengali families in the neighbourhood had got into two buses and taken off for the land of Kama Sutra.

I don't have many memories of the outing, except that I saw tall temples sprouting from large, green lawns and my parents buying a set of sculptures (for a family friend) which I had been forbidden from even looking at. But there are plenty of black-and-white pictures, taken of the trip with an Agfa camera, that stand testimony to my subconscious initiation into a world whose respected citizen I was to become years later. I don't know how families with adolescent children had dealt with the excursion; maybe they had opted out. I still preserve a souvenir from that trip: a black statue of Shiva which I made my parents buy as compensation for not letting me see the sculptures they had bought.

I SAW VIKAS OFF outside the hotel. Along with us emerged a posse of women—of different shapes but uniformly plump and decked up. A kitty party must have just ended. Almost each one had a car waiting, and the remaining few hitched a ride. After more than seven years of living in Chennai, I found it odd that jasmine flowers should be missing from their hair, but I quickly reminded myself that I was now on the other side of the Vindhyas.

Vikas took off on his scooter, promising to return in an hour. I strolled over to the Elite Chauraha. It presented a picture of the bustle that befitted an intersection of its stature. The shops were all preparing for the evening. At the *dhaba*s, cooks were expertly slapping small balls of dough into flat circles and baking them into rotis. At the *mithai* shop, *halwais*—cooks who specialise in making sweets and savouries—dropped raw *samosa*s into heated oil. Customers waited as they watched the *samosa*s being fried, glad they would be eating or taking home really hot pieces. Invariably, the sight of the *samosa*s being fried makes you hike the number of pieces you would have originally intended to buy. You might have set out from home planning to buy six, but when you see them being freshly fried you come back with ten.

For people who had gathered at the shop to buy *samosa*s, the evening had only just begun. They would go back home, savour them with tea, and only then preparations for dinner would begin—the women cooking it and the men waiting for it. For those already biting into *roti*s at the *dhaba*s, the day was coming to an end.

Elite Chauraha, at this hour, smelt of food—and diesel. What enticed me, however, was the delectable sour smell emanating from the cart of a *chaatwallah*. He was an old man who must have hardly had an idle moment ever since I spotted him in the shadows by the road. As I stood there debating whether I should walk up to him and indulge myself or preserve my appetite for drink, I noticed people stopping by his cart and gulping down *pani puri*s under the dim light of a paraffin lamp. I couldn't resist myself.

I had made the decision just in time: the *chaatwallah*

was now left with barely half-a-dozen of the crunchy shells that were intact for holes to be punched in. It was just seven-thirty, and he was already serving his last customer. There couldn't have been a busier *chaatwallah*.

I wanted to speak to him about the secret of his success, and maybe also about Jhansi, but the old man was way too reticent. His eyes clearly told me: 'There are other people to tell you about Jhansi. My job is to serve you *pani puris*. I can see you are happy with what you just ate. So pay and move on.' I paid him three rupees and moved on, back to the hotel where Vikas was expected anytime now.

As I waited to cross the road to get to the hotel, I wondered about the history of *pani puri*, variously known as *gol gappa*, *batasha* and *phuchka*. Did it exist during the time of Laxmibai, and if yes, was there any possibility of this *chaatwallah*'s great-great-grandfather being summoned to the palace, where he would be deftly punching holes into the crunchy shells and filling them with the tingling liquid before serving them to the queen of Jhansi and her friends. There is no way of knowing these things. Sellers of street food are too busy eking out a living to keep an account of their history.

I was enquiring about taxi fares to Khajuraho at the reception when Vikas returned. He advised me to take the bus. 'You can go for free. I know a travel agent who sends busloads of foreigners to Khajuraho everyday. I know him well. You just have to hop into one of his buses,' he said.

I didn't like the idea: I wanted to travel to Khajuraho, and not just be transported there. But I found it difficult to say no when he insisted that I come right away to the travel agent, whose office happened to be next door.

At the agent's office, however, no one seemed to know Vikas. He enquired about the people he supposedly knew, but none of those people happened to be around at the moment. Vikas, embarrassed that he wasn't acknowledged in the office of a travel agent he had claimed to know well, told me that it wasn't such a bad idea, after all, to take a taxi to Khajuraho. The hotel, he said, would ensure that I got a good deal.

We walked out to the main road. He said he was taking me to a *dhaba* where we would be having a drink. I gleefully followed him: ever since I moved to Chennai I had never been to a real *dhaba*, but only to popular restaurants that have incorporated the word into their signboards. I could have walked into one of the *dhaba*s at Elite Chauraha, but without interesting company—and a couple of drinks—such places can come across as soulless.

At the *dhaba*, Vikas was warmly welcomed by its young owner who was manning the *tandoor* on the pavement. 'What a coincidence that you came today. I am making Afghani chicken for the first time,' he said.

Vikas introduced him to me and we shook hands. His name was Jagat. He asked us to go in and take a table while he gave finishing touches to the dish he was trying his hand at. As soon as we sat down, I noticed a warning painted on the wall facing me: '*Sharaab peena sakht manaa hai*'—Drinking alcohol is strictly prohibited here.

'What would you like to have?' Vikas asked me, 'I don't drink much these days. I will take a little from whatever you are having.'

I said I wanted whisky. Vikas motioned one of the waiters—a young boy—to come over and I gave him the money. Vikas told the boy with an air of authority,

'Daudte hue jaana, haanfte hue aana'—Go running and come back panting. In other words, get it quick.

Soon we were drinking from steel tumblers, with the whisky bottle 'hidden' under the table. The idea was not to offend teetotallers who might be walking into the *dhaba* just for the food. But this exercise in secrecy seemed pointless because I could see most patrons taking measured sips from steel tumblers at regular intervals—something you wouldn't do had the tumbler contained just plain water.

Jagat placed a plate of steaming Afghani chicken at our table and sat next to me. It did not look or smell very different from the regular *tandoori* chicken. But then, I am the wrong person to be able to tell one variety of chicken from another. Anyhow, the Afghani chicken tasted great along with the electrifying mint chutney. I complimented Jagat profusely, partly because I meant it and partly because he had been genuinely happy to have us over on an evening when he was trying his hand at a new dish.

The *dhaba* used to be a 'tent house', supplying tents for weddings and other functions, until two years ago, when Jagat decided to fully exploit its vantage location on the main road. So a man who supervised pitching of tents was now grilling chicken. 'The profit is larger in the food business, provided it does well,' he said.

I asked Jagat if he was happy living in Jhansi, or dreamed of working in a big city like Delhi. 'Why, do you have a job in mind for me in Delhi?' he asked with utmost seriousness, perhaps mistaking my question for a veiled offer. When I clarified that I had only wanted to know whether he ever nursed ambitions of migrating to a big city to make more money, he once again asked, 'Why, do you have a job for me?'

I dropped the subject and asked him if he would like to have a drink. Jagat joined his palms into a *namaste*—the polite way of refusing food or drink in north India. He was a teetotaller, and so was his younger brother Bhagat, who had joined us now. He was coming straight from the coaching institute where, for two hours in the morning and two hours in the evening, he taught business mathematics and statistics.

From their appearances, it was difficult to believe they were brothers. Jagat was so shabby that he could easily be mistaken for a waiter at the *dhaba*. Bhagat, given the nature of his job, was smartly attired. He looked young enough to be a student himself and spoke with the swagger of a student leader.

I put the same question to Bhagat, about chasing a dream in a big city. He gave a general reply, cleverly keeping himself out of the picture: 'In a place like this, people don't aspire for too much. They are happy with what they have. If someone is earning fifteen thousand rupees a month, he is satisfied. He will say, "This is enough for me, why do I need more?" That is the mindset in Jhansi.'

Jagat was quietly listening to his younger brother, not inclined either to agree or disagree. They seemed like two brothers out of a Hindi film in which the elder one makes huge sacrifices and endures numerous hardships and humiliations so that the younger could become a 'big man' someday and fulfil the dreams the elder brother never got to pursue.

I tried imagining Bhagat, in his spare time, lending a helping hand to his elder brother in the preparation of Afghani chicken, but it was a scene I found almost impossible to visualise. Bhagat had arrived like a guest, and he left like one. Jagat returned to the oven to give the Afghani touch to more chicken pieces. Vikas and I returned to finishing the whisky.

So far, he had updated me about the boys in our school, and now, under the influence of alcohol, began recalling the names of the girls who were popular among the boys back then. But barring three or four he was still in touch with, he could barely give me any information about the rest of the girls, including those I would have liked to know about. He was clueless about their whereabouts and understandably so: during the time we went to school—and that wasn't very long ago—girls, after finishing their studies, were expected to migrate to a land called Marriage and become its faceless citizens. Tracing them was not an easy task.

Still, I got to know enough to reflect upon the rest of the night. The girl I would once dream of—a Punjabi girl called Sunita—was now married to a man who ran a small pharmacy back home in Kanpur. She had been elusive back then, but now, in hindsight, she didn't deserve to be in my dreams. Another girl, Sheetal, who was the heartthrob of all the grown-up boys at school, now attended to customers at the showroom of a cellphone service provider in Delhi. I would have loved to walk into the showroom, just to see how Sheetal looked like these days. Vikas, alas, did not have the details.

Vikas, the more I observed him, fitted Bhagat's description of the people of Jhansi—that they are content with whatever they have. On the one hand, Vikas had numerous complaints against Jhansi—murders were routine, streets were unsafe, development was very limited.

But on the other hand, his life had fallen into a pattern in this town, and he didn't seem the kind who would trade that pattern for a better lifestyle in a big city. He had a wife who loved him unconditionally and a two-year-old daughter who sought to seek his attention with her antics.

When I took a picture of the three of them later than night, they came across as one happy family.

THE NEXT MORNING, scanning the Hindi papers over a breakfast of *alu paratha*s and curd, I realised why Vikas had said that murders were routine in Jhansi. I read about three men who had been arrested for killing a bank manager in broad daylight after robbing three lakh rupees from him, and about a boy whose body had been found hanging from a tree. Incidences such as these were common in Uttar Pradesh, especially in the lawless outskirts of its cities.

Suddenly I felt like getting out of Jhansi and going to Orchha. So far, I had only seen pictures of the place—narrow streets subdued by imposing medieval buildings set against a blue sky—and been harbouring a desire to go there someday. The time was now.

Orchha, even though only 19 km away from Jhansi, belongs to the neighbouring state of Madhya Pradesh. Jhansi, it so happens, sits on the throat of the bitter gourd-shaped incursion that the border of Uttar Pradesh makes into Madhya Pradesh. If Jhansi were a human being stretching his hands sideways, each of the hands would be touching Madhya Pradesh. And Orchha, even though a stone's throw from the town, fell in the neighbouring state.

I called up the reception and asked them to get me a taxi. The idea was to be back by noon, so that I could devote the rest of the day to Jhansi. The bell rang and when I opened the door, a boy presented himself. He was to take me to Orchha, not in a taxi, but in an autorickshaw. I was a bit relieved: if an autorickshaw could take me there, the journey obviously was not going to be long and rough.

A sticker on the windscreen of the autorickshaw quoted an Urdu couplet:

> *Hum kis kis ki nazar ko pehchaane, sabki nazar mein rehte hain*
> *Kismat hi kuchh aisi payi hai, har waqt safar karte hain.*

It loosely translates as:

> I might not recognise everybody, but everybody recognises me
> Such is my destiny that I am forever on the road.

In north India, it is common to find public transport vehicles painted or pasted with couplets that urge you to look at the driver as a man who has a heart and not as a man without one.

The autorickshaw made its way out of the Jhansi traffic, passing through numerous poultries and roadside vendors selling eggs and meat, and was finally zooming away on a smooth, empty stretch of road flanked by villages and their vast fields.

Hardly a human was in sight except the occasional cowherd—and I was not even five kilometres away from

Jhansi. Once in a while, a roadways bus would storm past us, but that was about it.

Suddenly, the autorickshaw came to a halt. The boy driver had no clue why. He opened the tool box and, asking me to remain seated, started meddling with the engine. He fixed the problem and we were off again, only to sputter to a halt a few yards later. Once again he opened the tool box and went to the rear of the vehicle to open the engine.

These fifty-yards-at-a-time trips went on for a while till we were at a petrol pump, where he told me that something was seriously wrong with his vehicle and that he would send for another autorickshaw to take me to Orchha. He made a call—from my mobile phone—and asked me to wait. I did not mind.

I went across the road and stood under a tree and lit a cigarette. I could have spent the rest of my day there, if only someone had brought me a charpoy and a book and maybe the lunch that farmers eat when they are out on the fields. I have always been curious about a farmer's meal, but I think I know what he eats: five or six *roti*s with a little *daal* and a large onion. Or maybe just the *roti*s and the onion, if he is very poor. When you are toiling in the fields from dawn to dusk, you earn a meal instead of being entitled to it, and in such a case, even dry *roti* and onion becomes a delicacy. And if you happen to drop some pickle or chutney on the bunch of *roti*s, it becomes a full-course meal.

I smoked another cigarette, watching the odd farmer walking past. They were all unhurried in their gait, as if the world could wait while they sauntered from one place to another. But then, why should they hurry? They did not belong to the world where hourly deadlines had to be met. I was, however, getting impatient now. I went over to the boy driver, who was loitering in the petrol pump waiting for a mechanic. I demanded to know the status of the autorickshaw that was supposed to come. He made another call, from my phone (he said he was unable to make outgoing calls from his phone), and told me it was on its way.

Finally, two boys arrived—not in an autorickshaw but on a bike. They had come to take a look at the engine. I lost my cool, but stranded in the middle of nowhere, I could do little except raising my eyebrows in irritation. One of the boys suggested he could drop me back to the hotel, where he would get me another autorickshaw.

I could have flagged down a passing bus or a 'tempo'. But the speed with which the buses were passing, it would have been a challenging task to flag one down. And the 'tempos', without exception, were packed well beyond their capacity. And so, riding pillion and smelling the hair of a total stranger, I was back in the hotel. I decided to see Orchha on my way to Khajuraho, maybe the next morning.

The sun was too harsh now to be aimlessly roaming the streets of Jhansi. So what could I do now? Why worry, when there was Mehfil-e-Shaam, the in-house bar of my hotel?

I was, as I had expected, the only one in the bar. Behind the counter sat the bartender, drinking tea and watching TV. A Sunny Deol movie was on. A waiter appeared as soon as I took a table facing the TV. When I looked at the menu, I had half a mind to settle in Jhansi:

Single Malt Rs 70 (50 ml)
Royal Challenge Rs 45 (50 ml)
Simron Off Rs 50 (50 ml)

The rates dipped as one climbed down the list. Since it was afternoon, I asked for Simron Off, or Smirnoff vodka, along with a plate of green salad, Rs 18. For a while I wrote, jotting down my impressions of Jhansi, occasionally looking up to watch the scenes when Sunny Deol confronted the villain, Om Puri.

A couple of men breezed into the bar. They seemed to be in their early thirties and clearly were regulars because the bartender greeted them cheerfully. I was soon dividing my time between writing, watching the movie and eavesdropping on their conversation.

One of the men, who spoke with the aggression of a small-time don, did most of the talking: he was bragging about his visit to a minister's office in Lucknow. The wife of his friend wanted a teacher's job and he had gone to the minister to request him to put in a word with the school.

Meanwhile, as the advertisements came on the TV, the bartender began to surf channels and one of them happened to be showing *Sholay*. He paused for a moment and moved on to other channels. The man who looked like a don shouted, '*Kya kar rahe ho! Chalne do na usko!*'— What are you doing! Let *Sholay* go on.

So for the umpteenth time—but with no dissipation in the excitement—I was now watching Thakur's hands being chopped off by the cruel Gabbar Singh. And soon after came on the foot-tapping song, '*Mehbooba Mehbooba*'. No one took his eyes off the screen.

The don commented to his companion, 'This film must be about fifteen years old, but still a hit. Can you imagine?' His comment had a whiff of pride.

'Thirty-two years, not fifteen,' I reminded him, unable

to hold myself back because I too shared that pride. We both belonged to the *Sholay* generation.

THE FORT OF JHANSI was a thirty-minute walk from the hotel. It sat on a mound like a giant tortoise, but dwarfed by cellular phone towers that dominated the landscape around it—a perfect example of the past resigning to the present.

I had company in a busload of tourists from Tamil Nadu who had just arrived and flocked around the signboard that detailed the features of the fort. When I heard Tamil being spoken, I instantly felt at home.

Loyalty can be so disloyal at times: here I was, savouring the back-home feeling in the terrain of Uttar Pradesh after having lived in Chennai for seven years now, and yet, the moment I hear Tamil being spoken in the land I was born, I start feeling at home.

Loyalty was wavering at the same spot even in 1857, when Laxmibai, like many other native rulers, discovered that allegiance to the British no longer guaranteed her status as the queen of Jhansi. She revolted and, as the enemy forces zeroed in on the fort, escaped by jumping from the fort on a horse with her adopted son strapped to her back—only to die valiantly three months later, in June 1857, in a battle near Gwalior.

Her valour has been celebrated in a lengthy poem composed by local poetess Subhadra Kumari Chauhan, which is inscribed on a signboard at the entrance alongside the site map of the fort:

Khoob ladi mardaani woh to,
Jhansi waali rani thhi:

Valiantly she fought like a man;
She was, after all, the queen of Jhansi.

While in school, we were expected to memorise the poem by heart, but I pretty much doubt if any of us retains anything beyond these two lines. These are the lines that matter anyway.

I trailed the tourists from Tamil Nadu as they began their tour of the fort. I trailed them because there were unfriendly-looking monkeys all around, and I did not wish to be ahead of the pack.

Spread over sixteen acres, the fort, during those days, was a complex that combined the medieval-day equivalents of a luxury hotel suite, a multiplex, the prime minister's office, the Supreme Court and the central jail. Though it is quite impossible to imagine a queen frolicking with her friends in a garden that happened to be just yards away from a tower where those found guilty of grave crimes would be hanged.

The nit-picking monkeys prevented me from exploring the nooks and corners of the fort. I spent most of my time at the 'Jumping Spot', where Laxmibai had taken the leap from on horseback. I looked down the parapet and, somehow, the plunge didn't seem highly dangerous to me, maybe because I live in the era of Akshay Kumar who, in TV commercials, jumps from even greater heights in pursuit of a bottle of Thums Up. But back then, it must have been a dangerous real-life stunt, pulled off by a woman at that, that too with a child strapped to her back.

From the 'Jumping Spot', I could see the rugged terrain of Jhansi laid out in front of me. Right below the fort was a school, Laxmi Vyayamshala Inter College. And right ahead, on the horizon, the statue of hockey wizard Dhyanchand, standing tall atop a hillock. He belonged to Jhansi as well, and he too was a symbol of native Indian heroism, albeit on a different turf.

On the face of it, a sword-wielding queen and a gold medal-winning hockey wizard might appear to be belonging to two remote eras. But had Laxmibai managed to live till the age of hundred, which is not a biological improbability, she could have welcomed Dhyanchand back to Jhansi after his mesmerising performance at the 1936 Berlin Olympics.

But Dhyanchand, in spite of the larger-than-life statue in Jhansi, is neither relevant nor remembered in present-day, cricket-crazy India. Like the fort, his statue too stands dwarfed by the towers of cellphone service providers, many of whom have popular cricketers as their brand ambassadors.

When I came out of the fort, I was accosted by a hawker selling crudely-printed Hindi pocketbooks that told the story of Laxmibai. I bought a copy, for ten rupees. The front cover showed a smiling Laxmibai atop a white horse and raising her sword. Her son Damodar, tied to her back, also sported a hint of a smile. As if the two were setting out on a hunting expedition. On the back cover was an advertisement of another Hindi book, *Film Acting Guide*, printed by the same publisher. The line that was meant to seduce readers into buying the fifty-rupee guide went like this: 'Want to become a film star? If you really want to lead the glamorous and luxurious life of stars like Amitabh Bachchan, Rekha, Dharmendra, Shah Rukh, Sunny Deol, Dimple, Madhuri, Karishma Kapoor, Govinda and others, order this book today. It not only tells you how these stars became successful but also provides you with addresses of producers and directors.'

I was curious to know if people actually order this book and write to producers and directors or—who knows—even land up at the addresses printed in it. Maybe a lot of them do: fifty rupees is a small sum to buy fodder for your dreams. It is a different matter that most of those dreams must be remaining just that—dreams. The sun was beginning to set, and I walked back to the hotel.

As I stopped at the reception to claim my key, I found, to my surprise, the receptionist not acknowledging my presence. He was busy narrating to someone a corporate joke he had heard recently: 'And you know what the notice board said? It said, *Rule no. 1: The boss is always right. Rule no. 2: When in doubt, refer to rule no. 1.* Can you beat that?'

The receptionist laughed, repeating the two rules over and again—in halting but clear English. Only when the other man seemed to have comprehended the joke did the receptionist turn to me with his trademark politeness and hand over the keys. And only then I figured why he had been ignoring me all this while: he wanted me to stay there and listen to his joke and appreciate his sense of humour.

This was an intelligent joke after all, unlikely to be comprehended or relished by most people he spent his day with—certainly not his own boss who sat in an adjoining room like an alert snake, ready to strike on any waiter sneaking in alcohol for guests and thus hampering the business of the in-house bar.

While taking the keys, I asked the receptionist to arrange a taxi for the next morning: I would go to Orchha first, then Khajuraho, and back to Jhansi in the night. He immediately called up a taxi operator. A long conversation ensued between them, during which I heard him bargain on my behalf. Finally, hanging up the phone, he informed me, in English, 'The taxi will come at eight o' clock, sir.'

'Eight o' clock is too early. Can't you make it ten?'

'Take your time, sir. The taxi can wait,' he assured me.

I had begun to like him. I had begun to like my room as well. Once you spread out your night clothes and books and notebook and pen on the bed, any room starts looking homely and agreeable. And the bed in this room had spotless, clean-smelling white sheets and pillow covers.

There was nothing I could complain about as I lay down thinking: so this is Jhansi, where my father and my numerous Malayali classmates stopped by during their journeys down south. Jhansi, for them, meant a railway station with grimy wooden benches on which people waited for hours for connecting trains. For me, Jhansi was now an air-conditioned room with a clean, comfortable bed on which I was going to sleep and dream of my trip to the land of Kama Sutra.

SHARP AT TEN I walked out of the hotel and got into a car that went around the Elite Chauraha to hit the road to Orchha. Before the driver could permanently place his foot on the accelerator, we stopped twice: once to buy a pair of batteries for my camera, and again at a petrol pump where I was made to part with half of the decided fare so that the car could tank up on fuel. No interruption after that as we zoomed past the same fields where the autorickshaw had broken down the day before—and beyond.

At times trucks and roadways buses overtook us by a whisker, at times they approached us menacingly, as if threatening to blow us into smithereens but merely brushing past, again by a whisker. For the authorities, however, there were concerns bigger than road safety, as indicated by the signboard which sprung up as soon as we crossed over to Madhya Pradesh:

AIDS ka virodh, bus ek nirodh.

Condom alone can fight AIDS.

Driving through miles and miles of dull terrain, with hardly a human in sight to break the monotony, the use of condom was the last thing to occur to one's mind. The only female in the picture was the unseen woman whose unfaithfulness was being mourned by the songs playing loudly on the car speakers. One song after another dripped with the pain of a hurt man, and the singer's melancholic voice was doing full justice to the sad lyrics.

I asked the driver for the cassette cover and found the singer's name printed as Ashok 'Zakhmi'. Zakhmi: the one who is hurt. I was surprised, and yet not surprised. Was Mr Zakhmi a smart singer who was capitalising on heartbreaks, or was he really a hurt man who wanted to share his sorrows through his songs? There is no easy way of knowing these things, but he did have a vocal cord that could be directly plugged to a broken heart.

My relationship with the driver, Raju, was still that of driver–client. It was yet to shape into the camaraderie that is inevitable when you are travelling solo on long journeys, during which the driver is your sole friend, philosopher and guide. Without him, you are as good as a traveller lost in the desert.

But as of now, Raju seemed to be engrossed in the world of Mr Zakhmi and I had no desire to distract him with small talk, considering that the iron monsters were constantly overtaking and approaching us at great speed.

Soon we were on a dusty, narrow road that seemed to be leading somewhere. The sun was harsh, the sky as blue as it could be, and on the horizon, the odd building started appearing, starting with a quaint railway station that identified itself as Orchha. Then came the *paan* shops that also sold Kodak film rolls and Duracell batteries— the most definitive indication that you are approaching a spot of tourist interest.

Finally, we were flagged down by a wiry man carrying a pink bundle of receipts. He charged us ten rupees for taking the car into the town. After about a kilometre, another man brandishing a yellow bundle of receipts flagged us down. He charged us ten rupees as an advance parking fee. And then appeared the building that made Orchha recognisable to me: only a little later did I get to know that it was called Jahangir Mahal, built by the ruler of Orchha in the honour of the Mughal emperor.

We parked the car outside the rampart and I bought two entry tickets, one for me and another for Raju, the driver. That broke the ice between us. He was now my shadow-cum-photographer as we wandered into the large courtyard of the early seventeenth-century palace.

I had spent the first thirty years of my life in north India before I moved to Chennai, yet it had never occurred to me that I should visit places like these, or even the Taj Mahal, the logic being, 'What's the hurry? They are just next door. One can go there anytime.'

But the 'anytime' never comes. Now, as a resident of faraway Chennai, Jahangir Mahal was no less important to me than the Taj Mahal, and I kept posing at spots from where the grandeur of the palace would be visible in the backdrop. What I desperately wanted was a shot of mine taken with me standing on a balcony on the first floor and looking out at the river Betwa. But there was hardly any water in the river to be visible from above, and Raju was too unused to the camera to be of any help.

We walked over to the river, which was more or less a bed of rocks, with a warning painted on one of the rocks, '*Paani gehra hai*'—The water runs deep. The rocks, however, were being put to good use. For the local women they served as curtains as they changed into dry clothes after a bath in whatever little water was flowing, while local hotels found them extremely convenient to dry freshly-washed curtains and bed sheets.

I sat on the steps of the ghat, in the shade of a tree. It was quiet and peaceful. On the opposite bank, a young woman stood on a boulder, slowly removing her *saree*. At first I looked away: I felt as if she was watching me watch her, and it was as embarrassing as being caught peeping into someone's bathroom. But then I quickly reasoned that if she had no problems disrobing in public view, what was mine?

Once the *saree* came off, she undid the petticoat and pulled it up to cover her breasts, after which she skilfully removed her blouse as well as her bra so as not to expose her breasts even for a second. And here I was, pointlessly debating whether to watch or not. She was obviously a regular bather and knew how to protect herself from prying eyes.

When my eyes returned to her, she was already behind a boulder, changing into dry clothes. All I could see was her head. I suddenly noticed Raju. He was standing at a respectable distance, gazing at the horizon with his hands in his pockets. I wondered if he had noticed me look at that woman. The thought of it embarrassed me a little, but then, what the hell.

It was eleven-thirty. Khajuraho would take about four hours to reach, which meant we had to leave right away if I wanted to look through the erotic sculptures at a leisurely pace. Walking to the parking lot, we ran into a sea of people: hundreds were pouring in and out of a cluster of temples across the Jahangir Mahal. It must have been an auspicious day, or else the locals wouldn't have turned up in such great numbers, attired in their colourful best.

The centre of attraction, I learned, was the locally-renowned Ramraj temple, where Lord Rama is worshipped as a king rather than a god. He is even honoured with a gun salute on Ram Navami. I wondered how I could have missed such a huge crowd in such a small place. Maybe I was beguiled by the quiet that hung over Jahangir Mahal and the banks of Betwa.

I asked Raju if we would get too late if I stopped by at the temple. He nodded encouragingly and followed me as I joined a river of villagers into the precincts. All along the path, hawkers had set up their stalls—wall hangings, colourful necklaces and trinkets, bangles, garlands, vermillion, paintings, miniature idols and even *pani puri*.

There were curious crowds everywhere—the kind of crowd that swiftly forms when someone falls into a faint or meets with an accident. I soon figured the reason behind the crowds. It would begin with a group of foreign tourists, armed cameras and curiosity, gathering around a stall. Seeing them, a bunch of villagers would form a circle around them—just to watch what the foreigners were up to. Seeing the crowd, many more would come running, wondering what was going on: was there an altercation, or had somebody dropped dead? In the end, no one would know what they had gathered there for.

At times I watched such crowds from a distance, at times I was part of them. At the lawns of the temple, there was a mass picnic going on: it was packed with people sitting in circles around open lunch boxes. The lone *pani puri* seller by the lawn was kept busy by young girls who wanted to make the outing memorable. I was extremely tempted to have a few *pani puri*s, but it felt awkward to join a row of adolescent girls who were squealing with delight as the spicy tamarind water tickled their tongues. Moreover, I had a long road journey ahead of me and I didn't want to risk unsettling my stomach.

So I bid goodbye to the temple without visiting the sanctum sanctorum, for it entailed removing my footwear for which I had no time now, and headed straight for the car. Once again, we were zooming on the highway, with the voice of Mr Ashok 'Zakhmi' for company. It is better not to mess around with drivers when it comes to music. They know what works best for them.

Even though it was hot, the drive was rather pleasant except during the moments when Raju had to spit out the *paan masala* he was addicted to. With the car running at great speed, he would open the door slightly and lower his head and spit out the reddish contents of his mouth onto the road. For him, the act was as natural as brushing his teeth, but for me it was like sitting in a high-speed, driverless car for those few seconds. But I lived on to tell the tale.

This was not the most scenic of drives: in fact, the absence of scenery made one even more impatient about reaching the destination. But there were rare moments of surprises. Exactly at the point where the milestone announced that Khajuraho was still ninety-eight kilometres away, there appeared a river called Dhasan that took my breath away. Its bluish-green waters flowed serenely as we crossed the bridge, as if asking me to stop there for a while to admire its beauty. But I had no time: ninety-eight kilometres would take almost two hours to cover on the roads of Madhya Pradesh. Only a little later, when we were flagged down at a toll post, did I realise that we had been in Uttar Pradesh all this while and were now entering Madhya Pradesh once again after visiting Orchha.

All thanks to the protrusion that the boundary of Uttar Pradesh makes into Madhya Pradesh. I paid a road tax of sixteen rupees which, as the receipt indicated, was to go into the coffers of the public works department of the government of Madhya Pradesh.

I was still optimistic about making it to Khajuraho just in time to spend a couple of hours there when Raju announced that he wanted to have lunch. My fault: in my eagerness to avoid roadside food, I had forgotten that he needed to eat. So we pulled up at a *dhaba*.

A cricket match was on, and as soon as we walked in, the dhaba owner ordered out the urchins who had gathered there to watch the match on TV. Since I was in a hurry, I could have done with *roti*s and *daal*, but since the onus of feeding Raju weighed on my conscience, I had to politely ask him what he would like to have.

It was almost like a lunch date, with me showing him the menu and asking him to choose. He settled for *aloo gobhi* and *malai kofta*, while I asked for *daal* fry. When the food arrived, I found Raju putting spoonfuls of *daal* fry onto his plate and in return pushing forward to me the dishes he had ordered. So this was a lunch-date after all, and it was clearly going to take as long. Thankfully, the cricket match ruled out the necessity for small talk over the table. As Raju lingered over his meal, I secretly wished I had Ram Ratan—the boy-driver who had taken me from Mughal Sarai to Benares—for this trip. But only after eating did I realise I had been hungry as well.

'Not to worry, we shall be there in twenty minutes,' Raju assured me, as he emptied a post-meal sachet of *paan masala* into his mouth.

By the time a signboard announced that Khajuraho was only twenty kilometres away, the cows were already returning home. Every few kilometres, they would be lording over the road, sometimes in dozens and sometimes in hundreds, marching like weary battalions. Their commander would invariably be a sunburnt, weather-beaten old man carrying a twig for a weapon. At one point, Raju got down from the car to scold the cowherd and ask him to get the animals out of the way.

On any other day, I would have got down from the car to savour this most magical hour of a north Indian village:

the cow-dust hour, or *godhuli*, when the dust kicked up by homeward-bound cattle mingles—against the setting sun—with the smoke rising from freshly-kindled mud ovens. But right now, the sunset worried me.

Needless to say, when we finally drove into Khajuraho, the gates of the temple township had just been closed. They close customarily at six every evening, only for an hour though, perhaps to regulate the tourist traffic. And now it was six-thirty. Which meant I had half-an-hour to kill before I could look for a hotel, and a whole night before I could catch a glimpse of the temples I had last seen thirty years ago without knowing what they were famous for.

Worse, I had not come prepared to stay for the night: as per my original plans, I was supposed to be on the return journey by now. Maybe stopping at Orchha had been a mistake. Maybe I should have started early from Jhansi. It was futile to analyse the delay now. I went to a *paan* shop and bought cigarettes and asked the *paanwallah* if I could find a hotel.

'*Kaunon chinta ki baat naahin, yahaan aapko pachaas rupaye se paanch hazaar rupaye tak ka hotel mil jayega,*' he assured me—Nothing to worry, here you will find hotels from fifty rupees a night to five thousand a night. His assurance was encouraging but hardly useful. I called up my brother, also a journalist, living in Bhopal. I hoped he could pull some strings, sitting in the capital of Madhya Pradesh.

'But it is too short a notice,' he protested.

'That's precisely why I am calling you,' I told him.

'Okay, give me half an hour.'

He never called back, nor could I reach him. There seemed to be a signal problem. By now the gates had opened and we drove around a very quiet township, looking for a place to stay. I was trying to spot a hotel that did not look too expensive but at the same time was not the fifty-rupees-a-night type.

The one that I found seemed decent enough. The reception area was laden with a holy air because of the incense burning at the feet of half-a-dozen large portraits of various gods and goddesses, and the rooms were clean and well lit. The only disappointment was when the receptionist, on being told I was from Chennai, had to think for several moments before deciding on the spelling of the city of my residence, which he finally put on the register as 'Chine'.

But a bigger disappointment, rather a shock, awaited me outside: Raju informed me that as per the rules of his owner, I would now have to pay twice the agreed amount since I was going to effectively block his business for the next day as well. I had no choice but to agree.

So I now had to pay extra for the taxi, pay for the room in Khajuraho, and also pay for the room back in Jhansi. Not only that. I also had to pay for a new underwear, a toothbrush and a small tube of toothpaste, a disposable razor and a bottle of aftershave, a sachet of shampoo, a comb—all of which I set out to buy as soon as I had paid the advance to the hotel.

The hotel, fortunately, had given me the standard kit of Medimix soap and a towel. Wearing the towel I lay on the bed, wondering if I could get a drink. I badly needed one now. Since there was an overwhelming presence of gods at the reception, this didn't seem to be a hotel where one could get liquor or even send the boy to buy some. And since I wasn't carrying a book, I killed time going through the menu card placed by the bed over and again.

The card was bilingual: English and Korean, and there was a separate category of Korean dishes, one of them being the Korean *paratha*.

The bell rang, and I shouted, 'Come in!' It was the hotel boy, asking me what I would like to have for dinner. Before I could answer, the door opposite my room opened and a Korean couple stepped out. (One could safely assume they were Koreans). The man, in accented English, first asked the boy the way to the terrace, and then asked him if he could get some beer. At which the boy asked him, 'Which brand?' I knew I was in luck.

When the boy returned with my whisky, I asked him about the hotel's Korean connection. He said the hotel had a tie-up with a travel agency that dealt only with Korean tourists. I was tempted to try the Korean *paratha* for dinner, so long as it was vegetarian, but the boy said the hotel's kitchen was non-functional for the time being and that he would have to get food from outside. I ordered the standard Indian platter.

I DIDN'T REALISE WHEN I fell asleep, but when I woke up the next morning, I did realise the significance of an old saying: Whatever happens, happens for the good.

Even if I had managed to reach Khajuraho a couple of hours earlier the previous evening, my trip would have been extremely hurried and, maybe, incomplete. After that, I would have had to endure five more hours of the return journey, that too in the night.

But right now, after a good night's sleep, I found myself to be the very first visitor of the day at the thousand-year old temples of Khajuraho. The sun was yet to light up their spires when I walked into the compound after buying a ten-rupee ticket.

The place could have belonged to me: not a soul in sight. The plaque placed right after the entrance informed that there used to be fifty-five temples several centuries ago, 'but now around twenty-five stand in varying stages of preservation.'

This compound, which to my untrained eye did not appear to be much larger than a football field, contained only seven of those temples. Archaeologically labelled as the Western Group of Temples, these are the ones that make Khajuraho famous. Separated by lush green lawns, each of these temples sat upright like proud lions, waiting for visitors to come and admire it.

My first stop was the Laxman temple, simply because it was closest to the entrance. I climbed up the stone steps and walked around. In the early-morning silence, the countless figures on its walls almost spoke. And suddenly, in the middle of them, the image of an orgy—the central figures being a man and a woman who are standing and have their legs entwined. One leg of the man, however, has been cut off by the sword of time. I clicked away.

As memento, I also wanted a picture of myself standing below the erotic panel. I caught hold of a passing gardener—an old man who was unlikely to have held a camera ever before. It was kind of him to oblige, but then, each time he got ready to shoot, the camera would go on the standby mode, and I had to run to him to put it on.

He managed to take some pictures, but in each of them, the orgy was left out. Finally, in exasperation, when I demonstrated to him the angle in which he should hold the camera, he said with a grandfatherly frown: 'Oh, you want to include those statues! You should have said so.' His words made me feel like a voyeur caught peeping into a neighbour's bedroom.

The picture that the old gardener finally clicked was not bad, but it clearly reflected that the photographer was more comfortable holding hedge-pruning scissors than a camera. I thanked him profusely and let him go about his work. All this while, a young man had been watching the photo session from a distance. I beckoned him. He turned out to be a gardener as well and he was more than willing to take pictures. Since he could sense what I wanted, I did not have to beat around the bush while giving him instructions.

Within a matter of seconds I had half a dozen world-class pictures showing me posing against world-renowned depictions of sex. In sheer gratitude, I was about to give him some money when he said, 'Come, I will show you something. Come down this way.' I followed him down the steps and was brought to a halt in front of one of the walls of the podium where, with the flourish of an artist unveiling his most precious work, he waved his hand, 'Look here! Kama Sutra!'

For a moment I was stunned, and the next moment I felt a little embarrassed, and then I decided to look at the sculptures as a work of art. But it was impossible not to think of sex: the acts were taking place in every conceivable manner, and they were not always between a man and a woman, or a woman and a woman.

'Look here, he is doing the horse,' the young gardener pointed out. He took more pictures for me and then excused himself with a namaste.

After I had come to terms with what I just saw, I strolled over to the other temples: Kandariya, Jagadambi, Chitragupta and the Vishwanatha. The designs are similar: each temple erected on a high podium, and has a porch, a vestibule, a *mandap* and the sanctum.

If time has a smell, you can smell it in Khajuraho. The air in the darkened interiors of these temples seems to have remained trapped ever since a thousand years ago, and standing all alone in one of the sanctums, it almost feels as if the Chandela kings had performed an elaborate ritual there just the evening before.

I sat on the steps of the Vishwanatha temple for a while and watched a squirrel breakfasting on a fruit. Suddenly, there was a whisper from behind: '*Soovar waala dekhna hai?*' (You want to see the one with the boar?) It was the young gardener again.

I followed him back into the Vishwanatha temple and on the inner wall above its door I spotted an image of a boar mounting a woman. He pointed to another sculpture that was right on the wall of the sanctum: a man and a woman doing it what they call 'doggy style'. He did *namaste* and disappeared again.

By now the sun had risen high and I walked across the lawn. A group of Westerners had gathered around a smartly-dressed guide and listening to him intently. The guide spoke fluent English and from a distance I could catch certain words: 'Bestiality', 'homosexuality', 'vices,' 'illusion' and 'delusion'. When I got closer, I realised he was justifying the presence of the erotic carvings in the temples: 'When you enter the home of God, you should get rid of all worldly distractions—that's the message of the Khajuraho temples.' And then, like a chemistry teacher, he summed up: 'Lust converts to love, love converts to devotion, devotion converts to spirituality, spirituality converts to super consciousness.' I got the point.

I came back to the Laxman temple. That's where all the action was—on the stones as well as on the ground. Two Westerners—a man and a woman—came up and I could see they wanted to burst out laughing on seeing the orgies. But they wore their trademark practised, dignified smiles and moved on.

An Indian family arrived—two men and three women. The women, who looked like housewives, broke into giggles at the sight of the carvings. The men discussed the dynamics of the complex postures and that made the women giggle even more. One of them mock-admonished the men: 'Don't look at them in a dirty way. They are works of art.' One of the men said in mock shock, '*Magar yeh to ghodey ko chep raha hai!*'—But he is doing the horse! The woman laughed and punched him in the arm.

Loitering there and watching people reacting in their own ways to the carvings, I quickly composed a few lines. Who knows, they might come in handy someday:

> Wave your magic wand,
> turn us into stones.
> So that we get embedded
> on the walls of Khajuraho.
> We can make love in peace
> for another thousand years.
> The sun would not flinch at us

> neither would the rain,
> and no ugly human
> to cry, 'What a shame!'
> They would only gape and wonder:
> 'Does this pose have a name?'

An elderly Western couple arrived, holding hands. The carvings made them give each other a quick glance and they hurried past. Then came a woman—unaccompanied and Indian. As soon as she saw the images, she pulled out her camera, but the moment she saw me watching her, she put the camera back. That's when I decided to leave.

Outside, a hawker accosted me. He was selling postcards of the erotic images and pocket-sized Kama Sutra books. For memory's sake, I bought one book, titled, what else, *Kama Sutra*. Back in the hotel, I turned its pages. My eyes fell on the instruction:

'If a man mixes rice with the eggs of the sparrow and having boiled this in milk adds to it ghee and honey and drinks as much of it as necessary, he will be able to enjoy innumerable women.'

That was some food for thought.

NAVEL OF INDIA
ITARSI

IT WAS DRIZZLING the evening I arrived in Itarsi.

'Do you have a booking?' asked the caretaker of the Public Works Department rest house.

'I had spoken to someone who said he would be speaking to the SDM. Didn't the SDM call you?' I asked him. SDM stands for the sub-divisional magistrate, the representative of the government and the last word in a small town like Itarsi.

'He might have called, but the phone has been dead for two weeks.'

'I have the SDM's number. Should I call him now?' I suggested.

'Since you say someone has spoken to him, it should be okay. I will show you a room.'

The room was large and the ceiling so high that the building could have been double-storeyed. The bed sheet had a large circular stain in the middle, as if a bunch of people had eaten an oily meal directly off the bed.

I surveyed the bathroom. It was almost as large as the room. It had Indian- and Western-style lavatories and a separate urinal. The pipe descending from the urinal, instead of being buried in the flooring, hung several inches above an iron mesh, which meant that if you were to relieve yourself after downing a couple of bottles of beer, there were fair chances of the bathroom getting wet. The thought nauseated me; as it is I associated urinals with smelly public toilets. Even hotels didn't have them in their rooms.

I sat on the bed, careful to avoid the stain, wondering what to do next when there was a loud knock on the door. The caretaker had returned.

'Sir, did you get to speak to the SDM?'

'I thought you said it was okay.'

'I know, but if you could just speak to him.'

I called the SDM. Hearing us exchange pleasantries, the caretaker, who had by now taken a seat, stood at attention. The SDM asked me to hand the phone to the caretaker, who went out of the room to take the call. When he returned, I asked him if the bed sheet could be changed.

'Why just the bed sheet, sir, I shall change your room. The next room is better. It has just been vacated.'

The next room had a set of sofas along with the bed, whose sheet was not as stained. But I noticed fresh muddy footprints of the previous occupant on the sparkling floor. I followed them, and they led to the bathroom, right up the urinal, where the two footprints formed a neat acute angle. I preferred the stained sheet over the footprints.

'I think I quite like the earlier room,' I told the caretaker.

'As you please.'
'But is it possible to get a new bed sheet?'
'That's all we have, sir.'
'I see.'

There was an awkward silence. 'I will now get a bucket of water and keep it in the bathroom.'

'Why? Water doesn't come in the bathroom?'

'No sir. But not to worry. Whenever you need water, just tell me. I will get you as many buckets as you want.'

I reclined on the stained sheet, using a saucer for an ashtray and pondering over my future course of action.

IN BHOPAL, WHEN I had asked my brother to get me a reserved ticket for Itarsi, he had laughed. He said nobody in Bhopal ever reserved tickets to travel to a place as close as Itarsi.

At my insistence, he had gone to the travel agent but returned empty-handed. 'They were laughing at me. They wanted to know who this person was asking for a reserved ticket from Bhopal to Itarsi. I did not tell them that the person happens to be my brother,' he said.

Much against my wishes, I had set out for Bhopal station without a ticket. I had been asked to buy a 'general' ticket (legally valid only for unreserved coaches and, therefore, ridiculously cheap) and get into a reserved coach of any of the trains headed for Itarsi.

So I stood in a queue to buy a 'general' ticket and, for the first time in my life, came across a corrupt woman clerk. She blatantly asked for 'something extra' from the man ahead of me in the queue: he had wanted a last-minute reservation on a long-distance train.

She was a buxom woman, the kind I would have liked to have as a co-passenger. But she broke my heart by extracting money from a hapless passenger. She was nice to me though, telling me which train to take and asking me not to worry about travelling on a 'general' ticket in a reserved coach.

'*Train khaali hai, kahin bhi baith jayiye,*' she told me with a smile—The train should be empty, sit anywhere you please.

The train turned out to be nearly empty. I got into a reserved coach and took a window seat. The train started with a jerk. By then I had other passengers around me, including a group of boys. From their books and bags, I gathered they were returning home after attending college in Bhopal.

I was hoping that the ticket examiner wouldn't bother showing up in a train as empty as this, but there he was, asking for my ticket while ignoring every other passenger around me. When I showed him the ticket, he sat down next to me.

'But this is a general ticket,' he said.
'I know.'
'But you are travelling in sleeper class.'
'I know.'
'But you can't do this.'
'I know. You can charge me the excess fare. I am also ready to pay the fine.'

He looked at me with surprise. 'What do you do?' he asked politely.

'I am a journalist.'

'Next station is Habibganj. You can go to one of the unreserved compartments. They are also empty. Why pay so much?'

'How much?'

'Three hundred rupees. Wait, I'll tell you the exact figure.'

'I'll pay. No problem.'

I was itching to legitimise my ticket, no matter what the cost. I wanted to enjoy my journey instead of sitting like a thief and waiting for Itarsi to arrive as quickly as possible.

The ticket examiner was genuinely surprised that someone should be eager to shell out so much money when he could have gotten away with a small bribe of fifty or a hundred rupees—which I am certain he would have asked for had I not told him I was a journalist.

I could see disappointment writ large on his face as he wrote out the challan. For a quarter of that amount he would have gladly allowed me to stay on a seat that was vacant anyway, but now the whole amount was going into the coffers of the railways, doing neither of us any good.

Once the ticket examiner left, the boys, who had been listening to us, began to see me in a new light. When they bought popcorn at Habibganj station, which came a few a minutes later, they insisted on giving a packet to me. And thus began one of the most spectacular train journeys of my life as the train slowly pierced into the Vindhyas, the range that divides India into north and south.

During the past seven years, every time I have travelled from the south to the north and back, I have crossed the Vindhyas either under the cover of night or witnessed its beauty from behind the sealed glass window of an air-conditioned coach. For the first time now, I had a direct view of the carpet of forest leading up to the sky. From a small brick cabin, overlooking the rail tracks and the vast expanse of the forest, a sunburned man was waving the green flag to our train. What a lucky man, I thought, he must be breathing the fragrant forest air that was now hitting my nostrils with great force. Who knows, he could be envying the passengers of passing trains.

The journey through the Vindhyas lasted barely an hour. Soon the train reached Hoshangabad, the administrative seat of Itarsi, and most of the passengers got off. Minutes later, we were pulling into Itarsi. Even though I had passed this station during countless journeys, this was the first time I was reaching for my bag.

If you were to draw diagonal lines on the map connecting the opposite extremes of India, they will all meet at Itarsi. From here, you will find a direct train to nearly every corner of the country. For a station of such importance, it was a little disappointing to see its exterior painted in a gaudy shade of indigo. But then, who ever gets to see its exterior.

I had stepped out of the station to a motley crowd of rickshaw-pullers, passengers—and young men, smartly dressed, standing around their parked bikes. Later I was to learn that the railway station is their evening hangout.

The rest house turned out to be a stone's throw from the station. I had walked in the drizzle.

NOW SITTING ON THE bed that bore a large circular stain, I wondered what to do next.

I had three options. One, call Amandeep Batra, the journalist whose number I had been given, and pay him a visit. Journalism was his secondary occupation; his primary occupation was running a grocery store he had inherited from his father. Whenever time permitted or an occasion demanded, he would send dispatches to the region's highest-selling Hindi daily.

Second option was to take a walk around the town and eventually find a bar. Third was to send the caretaker to get some liquor and spend the rainy evening in the rest house. I decided to walk.

There are two things that make walking in a small town highly pleasurable. One, there is hardly any traffic to deal with. Two, everything that you see around is affordable—unless you are buying a car. And in a place like Itarsi, there are no shops that sell cars, though I thought I saw a shop that did. In a showroom right opposite the rest house, I saw two red cars behind its glass panel, gleaming under yellow lights. On a closer look, they turned out to be Mahindra tractors. Welcome to Itarsi.

Walking from the rest house in the direction of the station, I found myself turning left into a large road where all the action seemed to be. Almost every city and town in India has a Mahatma Gandhi Road, and this was Itarsi's. If you happen to live in a big city and are missing the simplicity of the 1960s and 1970s, this would be the road to take.

The *samosa*-seller is still the biggest draw, with a huge crowd of salivating customers looking at their watches, waiting for the *samosa*s floating in hot oil to be sieved out and transferred to the container that still has a couple of pieces left from the previous lot. Then the stationery shops, where you once made your father buy fancy erasers and pencil sharpeners. And the cloth stores, where the entire family would once walk in before every festive season and often end up buying identical shirt and pant pieces for the children. Not to mention the tailor, who would be entrusted with the cloth pieces: he would take measurements and then give you a delivery date—a date you would eagerly wait for.

This used to be the road of your life till the malls and supermarkets came along. Itarsi, even though it connects Delhi with Chennai and Mumbai with Calcutta, is yet to catch up with Levi's and Reebok. It still lives in the era of good old Bata and the roadside cobbler who mends your shoes every time the stitch comes off.

What really caught my eye were the barbers' saloons: they were just about everywhere, making themselves stand out with catchy and creative names such as Rakesh Hair Art. One of them had decided against using English words on its signboard, so it called itself Khushal Kesh Kartanalaya—translating to Happiness Hair Works. And none of the barbers seemed to be idle. They were all patiently lathering the faces of their customers.

It began to drizzle again and I covered my head with my notebook. But it stopped before I could look for shelter. On an evening like this, the middle-class Indian family either makes *pakoda*s at home or gets them packed from the trusted neighbourhood vendor. I was pretty much sure that one such vendor would be around down the road, or else it would be an insult to a town which was still so Indian in character. It wasn't long before I found one.

His cart was parked by a quiet corner of Mahatma Gandhi Road, but his popularity and the weather did not let it stay quiet beyond few minutes at a time. People kept stopping by for *magoda*s: some asked for a hundred grams, some two hundred grams while a few demanded five hundred grams. *Magoda*s are *pakoda*s made of *moong daal*, the ideal accompaniment with tea on an evening such as this.

People like me indulge in street food not only because we like it but also as an act of belated rebellion against parents and elders who had kept us away from it, warning us against 'germs', 'bacteria', 'jaundice', 'typhoid' and 'cholera'. Street food is a lot like illicit sex: you are tempted to have it because you are always told it is taboo; it gives you great pleasure and yet is looked down upon; and once you have discovered the forbidden pleasure, you want to return to it over and over again.

So there I was, standing at the *magoda*-seller's cart, waiting for his attention. If you went by his soiled clothes, you could mistake him for a beggar and never eat a thing touched by him. But if you went by the devotion of his customers, he was an artist who was too engrossed in his art to notice the batter and the oil staining his shirt. I asked him to be generous with the mint chutney when he handed me my plate of *magoda*s.

While eating, I could not help eavesdropping on the conversation between two elderly men who were already into their second round of *magoda*s. One of them had only recently bought a colour television, and he wanted to boast about it. He said, 'They show some forty to fifty channels these days, can you imagine? They are good for the general knowledge of the children.'

The other man was clearly not impressed and, between bites of *magodas*, he let it slip, 'The new mobile phone that my son has bought stores up to 250 songs. Can you imagine that?' The other man kept quiet: having discovered the connection between television and general knowledge only recently, he was way behind in the ladder to understand the storage capacity of mobile phones.

Eventually, they both agreed that technology was doing great things to their lives and they moved on after paying a collective bill of fourteen rupees.

THE *MAGODAS* HAD SATIATED my urge to roam any further on Nostalgia Street, and now I wanted a drink. I retraced my steps, back towards the station, and walked into a bar. Liveried waiters beseeched me like pimps. Each of them wanted me to sit in one of the curtained cubicles.

'Full privacy, sir,' they cried, pulling me in different directions.

I ignored them. I had come here to pull the curtain off Itarsi and not hide behind one. Moreover, it was ridiculous to offer privacy to a lone man who had nothing to hide other than his longing for interesting company, perhaps the buxom woman at the reservation counter in Bhopal. Had she been around, it would have made immense sense to sit in one of the curtained cubicles. But I could not even recall her face.

I waved the waiters away and took a table in the hall, under the gaze of a semi-nude mannequin who held aloft a hundred-watt bulb instead of the torch of liberty—the sole source of titillation for people who came to drink here.

At the table directly next to mine sat two Malayalis, their suitcases secure between their legs. At the table behind mine were two Marathi-speaking men who also seemed to be in transit. The table in front of me, however, was occupied by a boisterous group of gym-fit Punjabis who were not passengers but locals out to celebrate the evening. The bar presented the picture of a mini-India loosening up on liquor.

The song that played loudly on the speakers was in sync with the pace of life in Itarsi: *Yaad aa rahi hai*, the once-popular song from the 1980 film *Love Story*, which had long been consigned to the memory folder of your mind. The songs that followed were of the same vintage— songs I never thought I would be hearing in a public place again.

The only thing in the bar that reminded you that you were living in the twenty-first century was an advertisement pasted on the wall, showing a suave young man being served with Signature brand of whisky on a plane. The caption said, '*MD at 36*.' Everything else in the hall belonged to the era when only grey-haired were fit to be MDs, or managing directors, when career was a path that took its own course and not a ladder that had to be climbed with aggression.

While I was on my first drink, I found the man on the poster to be mocking me. He was drinking Signature whisky, and so was I. He was thirty-six, and so was I. But he was the MD of his company, served by a smiling stewardess, while I was an ordinary journalist sitting in a dingy bar and served by a waiter who was nice to me only because he expected a tip.

After I started on my second drink, I began to pity him: what a wretched life he led, plane-hopping from one place to another to meet business targets. Was he really savouring the drink he was advertising, considering his mind was constantly juggling with dates and data? Whereas I was a free bird, who had perched upon Itarsi with the sole motive of roaming around aimlessly and who was now relishing the same whisky that he was holding in his stiff hands.

By the time I ordered my third drink, the young MD was out of my mind. I needed company. I called up Amandeep Batra, the grocer-journalist whose number I had been given. Over the phone, he profusely welcomed me to Itarsi, but when I asked him if he would like to join me for a drink, he politely refused. He said he had some relatives over.

'Let's keep it for tomorrow? I am a very light drinker, but I will give you company,' he said.

The bar was now getting noisy. Hordes of men, carrying attaché cases, began walking in. They all had trains to catch in a few hours, but right now they wanted to tank up on alcohol and food. Much to the delight of the waiters, the curtained cubicles filled up quickly. Drinking behind a curtain perhaps gave the occupants a sense of exclusivity and importance. And over here, the curtain also served another purpose: every now and then, someone from one of the cubicles would use it to wipe his oily fingers.

I settled the bill and walked back to the rest house. I now found the large room with the oil-stained bed sheet far more agreeable. I wished I could invite my Chennai friends right away and have a small party in a town that derives its name from *inta* (bricks) and *rassi* (rope)—the two things that Itarsi was known for. Ropes are no longer made here, but the brick kilns still thrive.

AROUND MIDNIGHT, I DECIDED to pay a visit to the station. The horns of the passing trains had been tempting me for quite some time now. And so I was back on the same road for the third time in six hours.

Railway station! It can be the most frustrating place on earth and also the most fascinating. Right now it was fascination that was powering me as I made my way through a multitude of sleeping people and several dogs and a few cows to buy a platform ticket.

The platform was empty and silent: it resembled a wedding hall that was packed until an hour ago but now all the guests had left. But the silence turned out to be a lull before the storm. Soon the familiar female voice announced that the train from Amritsar to Nanded would be arriving shortly. Suddenly, a mobile food-stall appeared from nowhere. The two men who had pushed it got busy. One of them began to furiously roll out *puris*, while the started reheating the *chholey*.

The first set of steaming *puris* was ladled out just when the train pulled in, so that the passengers could see how fresh they were. Not many passengers were awake at that hour, but there were quite a few—most of them Sikhs on a pilgrimage to the revered gurudwara at Nanded—who seemed to have missed dinner. They all flocked around the stall, waiting impatiently with the money ready in their hands—the train would leave in a few minutes. I joined the impatient men, even though I did not have a train to catch.

IN THE MORNING, THE caretaker on duty was a man called Jeevan Lal, who brought me tea and a breakfast of *poha* and *jalebis*. I asked him if he knew any engine driver—someone who drove steam locomotives and who might have stories to tell from that era.

'My father was an engine driver, sir,' Jeevan Lal said a bit hesitantly.

'Steam engine?'

'Yes, steam engine, sir.'

His entire family, it turned out, was associated with the railways. His grandfather was a gangman. His father had joined as a daily-wager, whose job was to load coal onto the tenders of locomotives. After many years of service, he was upgraded as the driver's sidekick whose job was to shove coal into the furnace of the locomotive. A few years before he retired, he became a driver himself, even though he was allowed to take the train only up to nearby Khandwa, a town most famous today as the birthplace of singer Kishore Kumar.

Today, Jeevan Lal's brother also drives short-distance passenger trains. But he quickly added that the trains his brother drove were not very important.

'Can I meet your father?' I asked him.

'He died a few years ago. But I have seen him drive the steam locomotive. I must have been ten or twelve years old then. I remember him lifting a lever and securing it with a rope. That kept the engine on high speed. When he had to reduce the speed, he would release the lever and pull it down.'

'You know any other driver?'

'Let me find out, sir.'

I asked him about Itarsi. 'There is nothing here now, except the railway station,' he said. 'The steam locomotives were all dismantled and bundled away in trucks. I saw that happening in front of my eyes. So what remains? There used to be four or five cinema theatres. They have all shut down now.'

I asked him about places worth visiting in Itarsi. He strongly recommended a hotel named Neelam. 'You can have lunch there. It's the best place in town to eat.'

After he left, I ate the *poha* and *jalebi*s while flipping through the pages of *Raj Express*, one of the local Hindi papers. One of the stories in its features section gripped my attention. It was the story of Kela Bai, a housewife from a nearby village who had been bitten by a snake while she went about her daily chores. She fainted after the snake bit her and was rushed to a hospital in Bhopal where, in spite of the doctors' efforts, she remained unconscious. The panic-stricken family then took her to a village called Lasuria, where priests at the local Hanuman temple are known to revive victims of snake-bite by chanting mantras. Needless to say, they revived Kela Bai and asked her to return to the temple on the full-moon day, as a mark of gratitude towards *naag devata*, or the snake god.

Kela Bai returned on the promised date. But the moment she stepped into the temple, her body started to sway, just like a snake sways to the pipe of a snake charmer. Her mouth made hissing sounds and her eyes began to glow. Other visitors to the temple were alarmed at first, but they went on to pin down Kela Bai after being asked by one of the priests to do so. The priest, who was convinced that she had been taken over by the spirit of a snake, used his powers and entered into a public conversation with the spirit.

Priest: I command you to leave this woman's body!

Spirit (replying in Kela Bai's voice): I won't.

Priest: Why not?

Spirit: Her house is built on the tomb of a saint, and her husband has been defiling the tomb by coming back every evening after drinking alcohol and eating chicken.

Priest: What if the husband promises not to touch alcohol or meat again?

(Khelan, the repentant husband, promptly makes a public promise that he would never touch alcohol or non-vegetarian food again.)

Priest: Look, he has just promised that he won't touch alcohol or eat meat again.

Spirit: Okay, I give him a year's time. If he goes back to his old ways, no one can save his wife.

Kela Bai instantly found herself freed of the snake's spirit and returned to her normal self. She and her husband went on to live, hopefully so, happily ever after.

I found it difficult to understand whether the

newspaper actually believed in such stories to publish it so prominently in its features pages, or whether it was deliberately playing up the villagers' belief in the supernatural in order to deter people from taking to alcohol.

To be fair to the paper, it had also published the quote of a local government doctor who said that instances of priests treating snake-bite victims should not be taken seriously because ninety percent of the snakes found in India were non-venomous in any case. 'Such treatments are only psychological,' the doctor was quoted as saying. But his quote had appeared in a tiny box, alongside the quote of Kela Bai's repentant husband Khelan.

I wondered if the readers would believe Kela Bai's story or the doctor's explanation.

AROUND NOON I WALKED BACK towards the station, looking for Hotel Neelam. The hotel was supposed to be facing the station.

By now I had gathered that it was sixty years old, run by a local politician, and so popular that it now had branches in Bilaspur, Nagpur and Allahabad. The hotel was hard to miss. Inside, it resembled any other modern eatery that was very particular about cleanliness. The man who sat at the cash counter was busy on the phone. I waited for him to finish.

'Two meals? Okay. Coach number? S6? Okay. Seat numbers? 41 and 42? Okay. Please stay in your seats. The food will reach you.'

The phone kept ringing. The callers were passengers in various trains that were nearing Itarsi: they seemed to be regulars who preferred Neelam's meals over the railways lunch. Or maybe they just liked to exercise the option of hotel food delivered to their seats.

When I finally got his attention and told him that I wanted to see the owner, he pointed me to a smartly dressed young man who was overseeing the service. I went up to him and introduced myself.

'I want to interview the owner,' I said.

'My name is Rajesh. You ask me whatever you want to. I am the owner's man,' he replied and showed me to a table. 'Have you had lunch?' he asked me. When I said I hadn't, he immediately ordered a liveried waiter to get me a full-course meal.

It was apparent that this young man ran the show, but he was unlikely to give me the story I was looking for—possibly a rags-to-riches story where a man sets up a modest sweet shop which, over the decades, goes on to become a brand name. I had no choice but to put up with the oral power-point presentation of Neelam's brand manager.

'We have been around for sixty years. This shop has always been famous for its sweets and savouries. These days the food is also extremely popular, and that's because we are very particular about quality. It's not for nothing that we have got ISO 9001-2000 certification,' Rajesh said.

I asked him what it was about Itarsi that he liked the most. Without even pausing to think, he replied, 'Sastaai'—low cost of living. 'You won't find such sastaai anywhere else in the country. Take my word for it.'

But there was something that made him unhappy: more and more long-distance trains were doing away with their halts at Itarsi. This, according to him, had dealt a severe blow to the economy of a town that thrived mainly on passenger movement. All these decades, junctions like Itarsi and Mughal Sarai had served as refreshment rooms for the trains and the passengers alike. Engines would change, coaches would be cleaned, water would be filled, and repairs, if required, would be carried out. Passengers, meanwhile, would enjoy the break from the monotony of a long journey and become temporary citizens of the railway station—thus contributing to the economy of the town surrounding the station.

But in the twenty-first century, most long-distance trains have transformed into self-sufficient, mobile towns, providing you with everything you might need during the journey—from water to freshly-prepared snacks to sockets where you can charge your laptop or phones. Why stop at Itarsi—a town with a population of just one-and-a-half lakh people—where hardly anyone boarded these long-distance trains and which is rarely a destination for the passengers travelling in them?

The railways no longer need these junctions, but the towns that have grown around these junctions badly need the railways. With cities increasingly getting connected directly by newer superfast trains, these once-mighty junctions are like jilted lovers in the romance of railways.

'Even Tamil Nadu Express had done away with its halt at Itarsi, but last year Suresh Pachauri (a Central minister hailing from Madhya Pradesh) got it to halt here again,' Rajesh told me.

As we spoke, I noticed a fair and somewhat chubby

man taking the next table, across a glass partition. He must have been in his early forties, someone women might have found passably good-looking once upon a time. When Rajesh's eyes fell on that man, he stood up and cried, 'When did you come? How come I didn't see you! Anyway, you have come at the right time. I have another journalist with me. His name is …' Looking at my business card he read out my name.

Hearing my name, the man jumped up and extended his hand over the glass partition. 'What a pleasure! I am Amandeep Batra,' he said with great joy.

He came over to our table and we made small talk. I told him about the water problem in the rest house and asked him if he could find me a good hotel.

'Nothing to worry. I will make every arrangement for you, A to Z. When do you want to move in?'

'I don't want to trouble you right away. But may be by this evening?'

'Consider it done.'

We shook hands again and he left. I stood outside the hotel and smoked a post-lunch cigarette. That's when I noticed the dharmashala next door. From its façade one could tell that this was a piece of history—once upon a time an elegant building that was now falling victim to neglect because of changing times and tastes. These days, nobody chooses to stay in a dharmashala—the Indian equivalent of an inn—unless he is hopelessly poor or utterly stingy. But considering that India is never short of either, dharmashalas remain in business, especially in towns of Hindu pilgrimage.

They were all built by prosperous Hindu businessmen, sometimes as a genuine gesture of social service, sometimes as a soul-cleansing exercise, and sometimes as a way to immortalise their ancestors and, therefore, themselves. Whatever the case, they provided members of their community an affordable place to stay when they travelled, especially in the days when hotels were unheard of.

This dharmashala, the one next to Hotel Neelam, was not in such a state of neglect as I had imagined it to be. In fact, its occupancy rate appeared to be 100 percent, at least going by the tongue-lashing the receptionist was giving to a man who had come with his wife and a child in search of a room.

'*Kahaa na kamraa nahin hai,*' he snapped—I told you there is no room.

'*Kuchh kijiye,*' the man begged—Please do something.

The man and his family, going by their appearances, seemed to be living on the south of the poverty line.

'*Kya karen? Kamraa banwaa ke den kya?*' the receptionist shouted—What should I do? Get a room constructed for you?

There was no way of telling whether the poor man was being turned away because there were really no rooms vacant in the dharmashala, or because he was poor and—more importantly—looked poor. Whatever the case, Mahatma Gandhi would not have approved of the receptionist's behaviour; but then, the receptionist would have joined the dharmashala decades after Gandhi spent a night there—in 1933. This building was indeed a piece of history. The place where I stood not only bore the invisible footprints of Gandhi but also those of Jawaharlal Nehru and Rajendra Prasad, as testified by a pamphlet published by the government of Madhya Pradesh, which the receptionist fished out for my benefit.

The four-page pamphlet had reproduced the testimonials given to the dharmashala by Gandhi, Nehru and Rajendra Prasad—all handwritten in the Devnagari script. Gandhi, in his testimonial, expressed gratitude that the dharmashala gave him shelter and expressed happiness that it also gave shelter to Harijans.

The pamphlet had also published the Hindi translation of a letter written by Gandhi—in Gujarati—to Vallabhbhai Patel from the same dharmashala. Excerpts from that published letter (the translation is loose—and mine):

Itarsi 1 December 1933

Bhai Shri Vallabhbhai,
I am writing to you from a dharmashala in Itarsi at three in the morning. Meera Ben has gone to wash her face. After this we will have prayers. Immediately after that we will have to take the train to Kareli from where we will go to Anantapur. Yesterday we were in Betul and from there we took the train to Itarsi where we slept in this dharmashala.

I got your letter. How long can you keep protesting against whatever is being written in the *Times of India*? I keep doing whatever I think is right. I hardly get to read the newspapers these days. I feel that Hari [God] is watching every work that we are doing for Harijans. The power that brings lakhs of people together will one day lift the veil over falsehood. As long as we do not falter, it is as good as taking a dip in the Ganga.

I know your soul is always with me. Who knows, that is what keeps protecting me? Your heart is full of a mother's love. Did I not experience that in Yeravada? This quality of yours reflects in your letters every now and then, and no wonder you are always concerned about the well-being of all of us.

Do not worry about me. Do not worry about that what is happening. It is all God's doing... Now we are

> on the train. I am sure you will take whatever treatment
> is necessary for the ailment of your nose...

Nehru had stayed here only for a few hours in 1937, while on his way to Nagpur, and his testimonial is short and sweet. He had merely thanked the dharmashala for its hospitality, and so had Rajendra Prasad, who had spent three hours here while on his way to Allahabad from Wardha.

I asked the receptionist if I could take a walk inside. He had no objections. It could easily pass of as an Indian palace—minus the grandeur. Most of its rooms have been rebuilt over the years, but a few around its spacious compound remain the way they were when Gandhi had visited. No one seemed to know in which of these rooms he had spent the night of 30 November 1933. At the time, the dharmashala had been barely five years old. A plaque informed me that it was built in 1928 by 'Betul resident Seth Mishrilal, Meghraj, Dhanraj, Panraj, Kesarichand, Deepchand, Phoolchand Gothi.' People of Itarsi know it as Gothi Dharmashala.

When I walked out, I saw the poor man with his wife and child still loitering at the gate, perhaps hoping to win the sympathy of the receptionist who must be dealing with such people every day. Was he really a poor traveller who was in desperate need of a room, or a beggar who was switching towns and wanted to spend a night or two in the comfort of a dharmashala rather than the railway platform or the pavement? There is no way of telling such things, unless perhaps you are experienced—which the receptionist seemed to be.

BACK IN THE REST HOUSE, I went to sleep. I had seen most of Itarsi, at least whatever was worth seeing in this small town of one-and-a-half lakh people. I was woken up by loud knocks on the door. It was Jeevan Lal, the caretaker. He ushered in a doddering old man, who greeted me with folded hands and a toothless childlike smile.

'Sir, you said you wanted to meet a steam-engine driver. This man used to drive steam locomotives,' Jeevan Lal pointed at the old man who was now sitting like a twenty-year-old facing an interview board. Or, should I say, like a shy bride.

Having been shaken out of sleep, it took me a while to gather my wits, during which I noticed that it was dark outside. Six-thirty, the watch said. I asked the old man his name and age. His name was Mathura Prasad. He wasn't sure about his age. He said he had retired from the railways in 2001, which meant he should have been close to seventy, but his shrunken frame and the involuntary shaking of his chin made him look much older. He was hard of hearing too: Jeevan Lal had to repeat my questions loudly into his ear.

Mathura Prasad, from what I gathered, was not the regular engine driver I was looking forward to meet, but a driver's assistant who, towards the fag end of his career, was found experienced enough to take steam locomotives around the yard. Since Jeevan Lal had told him that I was particular about meeting a driver of steam locomotives, he began explaining the functioning of a steam engine. He talked about pumps and injectors and pressure gauges, all of which was Greek to me, but the eagerness with which he was explaining made him very endearing.

Since he had lived in Itarsi all along, I asked him how the place looked like back then—whichever point his memory could go back to. To my surprise, it went back to the days of the Second World War.

'There was a war going on against the Germans, and military specials would keep coming to the railway station. We were very young at that time. Those days, no one could loiter around the station. There were British officers all over the place and they were very strict. We would always hear them saying, "Buck up! Buck up!" Their women were very kind. Whenever they saw Indian children, they would stuff chocolates into their hands,' he said.

Mathura Prasad, however, remembered the date he had joined the railways, 1 February 1964, on a monthly salary of forty rupees. He said even though salaries were low those days, it was more than compensated by *sachchai* and *imaandaari*—truthfulness and honesty. Looking at his withered face, one would like to believe that he had led a hard life due to his truthfulness and honesty. He was the ultimate picture of simplicity and simple-mindedness. At the back of my mind, I began toying with the idea of giving him a few hundred rupees before he left.

'Itarsi was nothing those days. It was just a *basti* (hamlet). Today you cannot even walk on the road. I am so scared to go out. There are vehicles coming from all sides. And those days, people were kinder and more generous. Every shop would keep a sack of *phutaaney* (roasted chickpeas). Whenever a beggar or a poor man showed up, the shopkeeper would roll a piece of paper into a cone and hand him a generous quantity of *phutaaney*. No one was ever sent away empty-handed,' he said.

I imagined a hungry Mathura Prasad standing in front of a shop for a fistful of roasted chickpeas. I made up my mind to give him some money.

I asked about his family. He said he had two daughters, both were now married. He lived in Itarsi with his wife.

'*Ab to yeh mazey ki zindagi jeetein hain* (now he is enjoying life),' Jeevan Lal remarked with a mischievous smile, '*Khoob ghoomte hain* (he travels a lot).'

Travelling and enjoying life were the last things one could associate with the doddering Mathura Prasad, so I asked Jeevan Lal to explain what he had just said.

He said, 'If he doesn't travel, won't his first-class pass go waste? He is entitled to two first-class passes, one for himself and one for an attendant. So he keeps going to places of pilgrimage, sometime to Benares, sometimes to Dwarka, sometimes to Mathura. He can afford to travel. He gets a pension of seven thousand rupees.'

'Yearly?' I asked.

'No, no, monthly,' Jeevan Lal laughed.

Mathura Prasad grinned, his chin shaking as ever.

I almost fell off the oil-stained bed. For a man living in the smallest of towns like Itarsi, a man who had discharged his worldly responsibilities and who now needed very little, except maybe two-and-a-half meals a day, the seven thousand rupees were as good as seventy thousand.

It was my fault. I had been overwhelmed by his withered frame that I had forgotten that he had retired as recently as in 2001 and that his ex-employer was none other than the mighty Indian Railways. Now I had half a mind to extract a couple of hundred rupees from him so that my evening drink was taken care of.

As they got up to leave, Mathura Prasad told me, '*Babu, apnaa card to dijiye.*' He was asking for my business card. I gave him one.

'How could I have left without your card?' he said with his toothless grin, 'One of these days I will come to Chennai because I want to go to Rameswaram. That's the only place of pilgrimage I have not seen.'

AFTER MATHURA PRASAD LEFT, I called Amandeep. I wanted to confirm whether we were meeting that evening and if he had found a hotel for me. He said he had spoken to the hotel, the best in the town, and they had plenty of rooms vacant.

'I suggest you check out of the rest house right away and come to the hotel. I will be waiting for you there. It's a minute's walk from my shop,' he said.

Checking out of the rest house, I realised, merely entailed handing over the room key to Jeevan Lal and walking out. Stay in that government rest house is free of cost. Since I felt odd checking out without signing bills or reaching for my wallet, I tipped Jeevan Lal and asked him to share the money with the other caretaker who had checked me in the evening before.

I took one last, good look at the tractor shop—it is not often that you come across one in a city—and then retraced my path once again towards the railway station, to the road where Hotel Neelam and Gothi Dharmashala stood. Down the road, Amandeep was waiting for me at the hotel that I had to check into. We climbed up to the reception and I opted for the suite: six hundred rupees a day.

The suite was spacious enough to accommodate a bed as well as a seating area where sofas were arranged. The bed, decorated with cushions and bolsters, was circular in shape—something I had seen only in the movies. The bathroom was spacious and clean. But the best part was that the suite overlooked the railway station. It was the equivalent of staying in a resort in Kerala facing the backwaters. What the backwaters mean to Kerala, the railway station means to Itarsi.

It felt good to be reclining on a sofa with a drink after roaming the streets of Itarsi almost non-stop and sleeping on a stained bed. Amandeep sat on a chair opposite me. He was pleased that I was pleased.

Along with us was Sanjay, a young man barely into his twenties. He was the Itarsi correspondent-cum-photographer for a Bhopal-based paper. For him, Amandeep was some sort of a mentor. He sat there like an obedient disciple, trying to occupy as little space as possible.

'I saw you coming out of the station that evening. You were wearing a white shirt, right?' Sanjay said. 'Amandeepji did mention that a journalist was coming from Chennai, but I had no idea you were the one.'

That was the only contribution Sanjay made to that evening's conversation. He remained a listener as Amandeep told me about Itarsi and, in the process, himself. Every few minutes, a train would blow its horn, providing the perfect background sound to stories about a railway junction.

Amandeep said he had three hundred regular customers

who bought from his shop on credit. Of them fifty percent were railway employees and the remaining farmers. Salaried customers cleared their dues every month, while farmers paid him twice a year, often in the form of wheat and soya bean, which grow in abundance around Itarsi.

'Farmers always keep their word. It is the railway employees who sometimes find it difficult to pay. Their credit keeps mounting. The thing is, everybody wants to live a good life these days. As a result, they spend more than they earn and then run into huge debts.

'Almost every lower-level railway employee is neck-deep in debt. That is also because drinking is rampant. The other day, a railway employee was walking back home when he found a snake. He was so drunk that he caught the snake and said, "Tonight this snake will sleep with me." Next morning, he was found dead on his bed, bitten by the snake.

'Even women have taken to drinking these days. They drink with their male colleagues just like we are drinking now. They have no shame. That is not all, some of these women, in order to pay off the debts incurred by them or their husbands, get into immoral activities.

'I know a woman called Manju. She has been a customer at my shop for eight or ten years now. Her husband is a technician in the railway hospital. She used to be a nice woman, but of late I have seen her with strange men. She sometimes calls me at nights, and I can tell she is completely drunk.

'I asked her once, "Who are these men I see you with?" She replied, "*Kya karen bhaisahab, majboori hai* (What can I do, brother, I have no choice)." Imagine such a nice woman, fair-skinned, beautiful, ruining her life. If you look at her, you can't tell she is that sort of a woman.'

Amandeep's description of Manju was more titillating than informative, and I asked him if there was any chance of her coming over now so that we could have a chat. I perhaps asked him that because I was sure he'd say something like, 'No, I don't think so. It's too late for her to come.'

But, to my horror, he actually pulled out his phone and dialled her number. The call went through.

'Manjuji? Manjuji? Yes, can you hear me? Manjuji, I have a friend who has come from Chennai. He is writing an article on how women get into the wrong path because they have to clear debts...'

I wished I had a device that could make me vanish from that room instantly. I was so overcome with embarrassment—which in hindsight was uncalled for—that I could feel my ears turning hot and my fingers trembling.

'He has come from Chennai. And he wants to... Manjuji, can you hear me?' The call got disconnected. 'Did you see that? She is completely drunk! She can't understand a word of what I am saying!' Amandeep was angry.

'No problem at all. I was only curious. Now let it be,' I told him.

'Let her come to the shop next time. I will give her a piece of my mind,' Amandeep fumed, putting the phone back into his pocket.

To change the subject I asked him how old his shop was. He took a sip of whisky and said, 'My father set it up way back in 1964 or 1965. He never wanted me to sit in the shop. But he died suddenly in 1984, and I had no choice. People owed us lakhs of rupees, but all those people disappeared after his death. I had to start from scratch, with a loan of twenty thousand rupees from the bank. All my life, I would remain grateful to the manager who helped me get the loan. But for him, I might have been on the streets.'

It was also in 1984, shortly before his father's death, that he decided to be a journalist. He was in college then, and he would often be sent by his father to collect payments from a certain Mr M, who at the time ran a highly prosperous sweet shop in Itarsi. Apart from running the shop, Mr M—who according to Amandeep was a very handsome man—was also a part-time journalist and nursed ambitions to become an actor.

'One evening when I went to his shop, I saw him giving news over the phone. There had been some sports event in Itarsi, and he was dictating the score to the head office. You won't believe how fascinated I was by the whole thing. I told him I also wanted to become a journalist. He asked me, "*Beta*, are you serious?" I told him I was. He wrote a letter to the owner and asked me to go and see him.'

But the gates to his ambition were not to open so easily. And then his father died. In spite of the setback and the sudden responsibility to look after the shop, he kept his ambition alive. He started taking tuitions in English language and enrolled for a long-distance course in creative writing. It took him a few more visits to Bhopal, where the paper was headquartered, to get the job.

The job, by way of money, meant nothing. But Amandeep was more than happy with the press card and the authorisation he had got from the paper to send news from Itarsi, just like his mentor Mr M would.

'I took English tuitions for ten years. I was crazy about mastering the language. Even when I got married, in 1990, I would go for the tuitions on my bicycle every morning at six. Even during the winters,' Amandeep said.

What happened to Mr M, the handsome proprietor of the sweet shop who had inspired Amandeep to become a journalist?

'He went to Bombay to try his luck in films. He even managed to get a break in a film, and I am told he spent his own money—fifty lakh rupees—on the making of that film. But when the film was released, he discovered that he had only a five-minute role. Moreover, it flopped. He never recovered from the setback. His shop closed down and he got heavily into drinking and died.'

THE NEXT MORNING SANJAY, Amandeep's protégé, came to the hotel. It had been decided the night before that he would take me to the railway yards and other places I might not have seen.

In the absence of Amandeep, Sanjay had transformed from being subservient to friendly. Before setting out, we had tea together. I told him that I was surprised to learn that Mahatma Gandhi and Jawaharlal Nehru had stayed in Itarsi, in the Gothi Dharmashala.

'Even Subhas Chandra Bose stayed there,' he said.

'Really?'

'Yes. And there he took ill. He was taken to the Mission Hospital. The ambulance which carried him there is still parked at the hospital.'

The hospital was only a few minutes away from the hotel. Parked in its compound was the skeleton of the ambulance—a 1930s or 1940s version of the present-day SUV. Except the steering, the gear handle and its aluminum body, everything else had been eaten to the bone. One didn't need an expert's eye to see that the vehicle had been parked there for several decades. But for the skeleton, it had become part of the vegetation in the hospital's compound—perhaps a car-shaped plant?

Sanjay and I then took off, on his bike, to see the railway yards. He did not want me to return empty-handed from Itarsi and used all his influence, as a reporter, to get me into places where ordinary mortals are either not interested to get in or allowed in.

These are places where locomotives, diesel as well as electric, are repaired— as if they were cars waiting in a garage for servicing. When you take a train, rarely do you realise that it takes an army of several hundred engineers and technicians to keep the engine in running condition. That way, this visit was an eye-opener. But what I enjoyed most was the ride to these yards—passing through kilometres of open space whose monotony was broken, every now and then, by the old-fashioned, single-storey quarters of the railway employees. They might be living in an island where there are no malls or supermarkets, but all of them have a tiny garden and an ample backyard. More importantly, they all breathe clean air.

As we headed back to the bustle of Itarsi town, it started to rain. Sanjay stopped his bike and we took shelter in the bus stop of one of the railway colonies. A few women who had just picked up their children from the school had already taken refuge there—and so had a couple of goats. As soon as the rain trickled down, the two goats moved out of the bus stop and began mating. One of the women, who perhaps didn't want her child to ask uncomfortable questions later, hit the mounted goat with a twig that was lying around. The animals dispersed like scared cockroaches.

Back in town, Sanjay took me to meet a senior railway officer. He was a genial man, who said he would be retiring soon, and happily so. 'Enough is enough,' he smiled. 'Now I will spend the rest of my life travelling. I don't know if I will ever go abroad, but I got my passport today.' He pulled out the shiny passport from an envelope and showed it to us.

When he learnt that I was from Chennai, he said, 'Most of the wheat and soya bean that you get in the south comes from Itarsi. Did you know that?'

He told us more: that one hundred and eight trains passed through Itarsi every day, and that about six thousand people in the town were employed by the railways, and that eight thousand passengers took trains from Itarsi daily, bringing four-and- a-half lakh rupees to the railways per day.

On the walls of his office were pictures taken during visits by various railway ministers and senior officers. In most pictures he was instantly recognisable, but in some of the older ones you had to look for him even though he was there, sharing the frame with the visiting dignitary. The hair, perhaps, made all the difference: he had it then, but not now.

These pictures, in a sense, were the sum total of his career that was now coming to an end. But then, he would be enjoying a handsome monthly pension, not to mention the two first-class passes.

'Don't go by his looks,' Sanjay told me as we came out

of his room. 'He is a very corrupt man. He owns half a dozen houses in Itarsi alone. And you saw the passport, right? Now he will spend his ill-gotten wealth in travelling around the world.'

Sanjay's father too worked in the railways. He didn't tell me about the nature of his father's job, neither did I ask. He had died two years ago, leaving behind two young sons, Sanjay being the elder. As per the age-old humanitarian practice followed by the railways, Sanjay could have easily got a job in his father's place, but he had stepped aside and got his younger brother's name registered instead.

'My brother is a very nice boy, but he also gets carried away easily. He is not calm like me. He often falls into bad company and they make him do things that might land him in trouble someday. If he ever lands in jail, his life will be finished. So he needs this railway job more than I do. We are just waiting for him to finish college,' he said.

Sanjay represented the storybook Indian who is known for sacrifice and hospitality. I had just learnt about his sacrifice, and I had been a recipient of his hospitality ever since the morning: he had no reason to waste his time on me, yet he had been taking me around on his bike, as if the assignment was more important to him than me. Neither did I live in north India nor did I work in a respectable Hindi newspaper to help him get a better-paying job. It was purely Indian hospitality at play. There was more to come. When I suggested that we go back to my hotel for lunch, Sanjay put his foot down. He insisted on taking me to his favourite *dhaba* for lunch.

'Trust me, they make the best food in Itarsi,' he insisted. When I agreed, he extracted a promise: that I should let him pay for the food. 'You have come to Itarsi, so you are the guest,' he said.

I ordered only *roti*s and *daal*, keeping in mind that he would be paying. Sanjay could perhaps sense that, because when the waiter turned to him, he ordered the best dishes and also two soft drinks. I looked around: most people eating there were, again, passengers in transit.

The waiter soon brought the soft drinks as well as the customary plate of chopped onions, lemon and chilli—an indication that food was to come soon. Just then, my phone rang. It was Amandeep.

'Sirji, where are you?'

I told him.

'Remember I was talking about Manju last night?'

'The one who...'

'Yes, yes, the same Manju,' he said, without even waiting for me to finish my sentence. 'Manjuji is here now, at my shop. I have told her about you. You want me to send her to the *dhaba*?'

'Okay,' I replied. Nothing else occurred to me at the time.

I felt my ears going red again and my feet somewhat trembling. I told Sanjay that she was coming, but he displayed no emotion. He said he had seen her several times at Amandeep's shop, but didn't volunteer further information. I too hesitated to ask—he was far too young.

The food arrived before Manju did. We were into our third set of *roti*s when I noticed two women standing outside the *dhaba*. The customers had already begun giving them glances. One woman was fair, somewhat short and slightly plump, and the other tall, dark and lanky. Neither of them looked any older than thirty-five.

'Is she the one?' I asked Sanjay.

He turned around to take a look and said, 'Yes, the fair one is Manju.'

'What do we do now? Should I go and call them in?' I asked.

'You wait here,' Sanjay said, 'I'll go and get them.'

Manju sat next to me, and the tall, dusky woman next to Sanjay. The uneasy silence that hung over the table made it impossible for me to swallow the food. Moreover, all the eyes were on us: some stared directly, while the others stole glances. I took inspiration from Sanjay: he was calmly eating his food as if nothing had happened. So I ordered four more soft drinks and opened the conversation, like a detached journalist.

I said, 'Amandeep was telling me that...'

Manju kept staring ahead. Beads of sweat formed on her neck. Hers was a very familiar face: she could have easily been the pleasant-looking sister-in-law in one of the TV serials who was now sitting at a family dinner with a strict father-in-law at the head of the table.

I said, 'Well, Amandeep was telling me that...'

She and the dusky woman exchanged glances and smiled.

I said, 'Last night, I was talking to Amandeep about Itarsi and its people, and he told me how...'

Manju was not even making eye contact. She kept smiling at her companion. Sanjay was busy eating. I decided to be direct.

'Manjuji, I am told that you used to be a nice woman but now you are doing certain things that a woman like you should not be doing. So I was wondering what could be the circumstances that forced you into such things.'

'*Majboori thi*,' she said—I had no choice.

When I asked her why, she narrated her story—her version of it.

Manju was very young when she was married to a hospital technician who, by then, already had a grown-up son from his previous marriage. The son fell in love with a girl from a different caste. They wanted to get married, but the girl's parents were strongly against such a marriage. The girl eloped with the boy and got married. Her parents filed a complaint with the police, claiming the boy had abducted a minor (which the girl wasn't). After a few days, the boy brought the girl home, where Manju treated her like her own daughter-in-law even though she was the wife of her stepson. One day the police came knocking and arrested Manju and her husband for keeping a minor girl in captivity. They were put in jail. In order to fight the case, they had to spend a lot of money and ran into huge debts. In order to clear those debts, she was now into prostitution.

'Is she your friend?' I asked Manju, pointing to the dusky woman.

'Yes, we met in jail and that's where we became friends. Ever since we decided that whatever we do, we will do it together.'

'Why were you in jail?' I asked the dusky woman.

She quickly replied that her story was the same as that of Manju's. She didn't want to elaborate. She was eager to leave.

'*Didi*, let's go,' she told Manju.

But Manju, having told her story, was in no hurry to leave. I could not decide whether to take her story with a pinch of salt, but it appeared that she was into this business out of compulsion.

It was somehow heartbreaking to think of Manju as a prostitute. She could have easily used her housewifely good looks to find alternative ways of earning money, such as impressing a middle-aged bank manager into giving her a loan and starting a small business. Maybe she wanted easy money.

What was even more heartbreaking was that she hadn't found a client since the morning. '*Subah se ghoom rahen hain. Magar koi nahin mila. Na mujhe, na isey,*' she laughed—We've been roaming since the morning, but no luck. Neither have I found did a client, nor has she.'

The dusky woman clearly didn't like being dragged into that remark. She reminded Manju, '*Didi*, let's go.'

Manju paid no heed. She was still lingering over her soft drink. A bit emboldened by now, I asked Manju how much she charged her customers. She laughed and looked at the dusky woman, who was not at all amused.

'I usually ask for five hundred rupees. But some men are such crooks that even after doing everything, they pay only two hundred. What can you do? You are not there to pick up a fight with them. You have people waiting at home. So you take whatever they are willing to give and come back.'

'*Didi*, let's go,' her companion said firmly.

So Manju was gone. This was a strange encounter: people usually spend an hour with a human being who had turned into a prostitute, but I had just spent an hour with a prostitute who was also a human being.

WHEN I RETURNED TO my plate, I found that the *roti* had gone hard. Seeing me struggle to tear it, Sanjay remarked, 'I kept reminding you to finish it before it gets cold. Should I order another?'

'No, I'm done,' I said.

I did not remember Sanjay asking me to finish my food. I did not even remember that he had been there all this while.

He paid the bill, in spite of my protests. He was still not done. 'Come, I will take you to a place where you get everything, from a needle to a dish antenna.'

SOON WE WERE ON the highway that led to Hoshangabad. For kilometre after kilometre, there was nothing around us except green fields. Suddenly, on the horizon, a large grey-and-blue structure appeared. At the first glance, it resembled an aircraft hangar. Must be a godown for crops, I thought.

'That's the big market I was talking about,' Sanjay pointed to the structure, 'where you get everything, from a needle to a dish antenna.'

As we got closer to the building, I tried to visualise what it must be looking like from the inside, but found it impossible to imagine a market that sold merchandise as varied as this, that too in a place where there was nothing around but miles and miles of agricultural land. All I could imagine was a hall where villagers would have their wares spread out on jute mats, selling needles and dish antenna just like they sold potatoes and tomatoes.

Only when we arrived at the building that I realised it was a hypermarket. Since Sanjay, who was unlikely to have seen even a supermarket, did not have a word to describe the place, he had kept using the needle-to-dish-antenna metaphor.

In keeping with its location, the hypermarket has been christened Chaupal Sagar—*chaupal* means a village club.

The mart is run by ITC, the tobacco major which, ever since smoking began to be looked down upon, diversified itself into the business of apparel and ready-to-eat packaged food. John Players, ITC's lower-end brand of apparel whose ambassador is Hrithik Roshan, sells its products here at a discounted rate. A decent pair of jeans is available for three hundred and fifty rupees. A sturdy pair of running shoes for less than a thousand rupees. From curtains to crockery, from underwear to umbrellas—there was everything. Not to mention the dish antennae from Tata Sky.

One product I thought looked out of place in that mall was the hairstyling gel. But then, why not: you can't keep on imagining villagers to be people who toil under the sun wearing a headgear. If Tata Sky has reached the villages, so must have the commercials in which cricket star Mahendra Singh Dhoni promotes a particular brand of hair gel. And when a popular cricketer promotes something, the line between urban and rural markets vanishes automatically.

I was tempted to buy a pair of jeans and shoes. But I reasoned: if I invested a couple of thousand rupees more, I could own a Levis and a Reebok instead, so why lug these all the way back to Chennai? Eventually, I settled for a tin of olive oil. While travelling from Chennai in the train, I had read an article about the wonders that olive oil can do to your body.

At the billing counter, I found myself behind a short queue of women from nearby villages. They were all carrying their purchases in the mall's shopping baskets. As I waited for my turn, I wondered if one of them could be Kela Bai, the woman who had been possessed by the spirit of a snake.

FROZEN IN TIME

GUNTAKAL

CHENNAI'S CENTRAL STATION, like humans, smells the freshest early in the morning—a smell you can relish only if you have not hurried in, which is rarely the case with people like me.

But that morning I made it well in time to stroll through the sea of humanity that smelt of fresh jasmine and talcum powder. The crates of fish had not arrived yet.

Standing at the door of my coach, I went through the reservation chart repeatedly—an old habit—first to make sure my name was there, and then to scan the names of my co-passengers and draw mental pictures of them with the help of their mentioned ages and gender.

I also had the time to keep glancing at the nameplate of the train. This was no ordinary train after all. This was the train to Bombay, the city where one went to pursue starry dreams and where such dreams, more often than not, came true provided you knew how to make a cocktail out of luck and labour.

Nearly every actor who has reigned over Hindi filmdom—from Dev Anand to Amitabh Bachchan—had once upon a time, from some city or the other, as a faceless passenger, taken the proverbial 'train to Bombay'. And today I was going to take the same train—from Chennai. Only that I wasn't looking to be a film star, for that matter I wouldn't be travelling all the way to Bombay: I would be getting down at Guntakal, a railway junction on the south-western edge of Andhra Pradesh which, for decades, has been serving as the transit point between west India and south India.

If you have been a regular traveller between, say, Bombay and Chennai during the era when air travel wasn't as cheap as it is today, a longish halt at Guntakal junction is bound to be part of your personal folklore.

Since I had never been on this route before (for that matter, never been to Bombay, except on a twenty-four-hour visit when I had flown in and flown out), I had bought a ticket for the non-air-conditioned class. The idea was to stare out of the window as the train cut across the Indian peninsula, south to west. A great sense of excitement overtook me when the train started with a jerk.

THE AROMA OF FRESH *IDLIS* took over soon after the train started. It was seven o' clock, breakfast time. The passengers to my right—a young couple with two young children—opened plastic boxes of Ratna Café, the famous chain of restaurants that takes pride in its *idli-sambar*. The passengers to my left—an elderly man and his daughter—opened two round steel boxes. One box was stuffed with *idli*s, and the other contained mint chutney. People sitting in my front removed the lid off the breakfast boxes they had bought at the Chennai station: each box had three *idli*s and a *vada*. I bought my *idli*s—four of them—from the pantry-car vendor. I had wanted to buy six, but I did not want to be seen eating so many *idli*s.

The *idli* has always been one of my greatest weaknesses. There was a time when I could polish off twelve *idli*s in one go, and then wait for a few more as my mother would put the next lot into the cooker. And I would have the steaming *idli*s without any accompanying dish—the steam would more than compensate for chutney or *sambar*. But then, those were my growing years.

To come back to the journey: the train had now picked up speed and hills started appearing on the horizon. But before you could fix your gaze on them, the hills would be suddenly gone and replaced by lush green fields. And then they would reappear after a while and disappear again. Then it came upon a short stretch where, when you looked out of the left window, you saw the brown of barrenness, but when you looked out of the right window, the greenery of the fields dazzled your eyes. The train ran like an animal that had lost its way in the confusing topography and was desperately trying to find its way out.

I spent some time sifting through a large collection of pirated, multi-movie DVDs which a hawker went around dropping in bunches on the laps of passengers. To my great surprise—and pleasure—I found among the pile a music video of ABBA, which I bought instantly, for thirty rupees.

After that I pulled out Paul Theroux's *The Great Railway Bazaar* from my rucksack and began to read. I had bought the book seven years ago, and had already read it a couple of times, cover to cover. But right now the same book with its yellowing pages held a special lure for me: it bore the autograph of Paul Theroux, whom I had met two weeks before in Chennai.

Since he was passing through the city, he had been invited by the American consulate to hold a workshop for aspiring travel writers. I had attended the workshop, not as an aspiring writer but as an 'observer' along with three fellow journalists.

When I had reached the consulate that morning carrying four of Theroux's books that I possess, the security staff refused to let me in with them. What if there were bombs hidden in beautiful prose? Finally, a member of the consulate staff, who happened to be a former colleague, arrived on the scene and saw to it that I was allowed in with all the books.

It was, however, a little disappointing to see Theroux in flesh and blood. A travel writer, in my romantic notion, is never seen in public. He is always inaccessible to his readers, busy collecting material in a faraway, godforsaken land which you might never visit in your lifetime except through his books. He is not the one you would like to be face-to-face with: if you see him in real, you could end up looking for flaws in his personality that might take away from the flawlessness of his prose. Gods are best unseen.

But who knows, maybe Theroux was not making a public appearance after all. Maybe he was visiting, rather revisiting, a faraway, godforsaken land called Chennai, and the participants of the workshop were only going to provide him with material for his next book.

Whatever the case, Theroux's personality did not match his prose. He came across to me as a bowl of bland soup. He was like the benign uncle in the family who religiously went for walks every morning and had dinner sharp at eight and who never went on a trip unless it was planned well in advance and to the last detail. There was nothing to suggest, as he gave writing tips to the participants, that he had been a globe-trotter in the literal sense of the word. But then, appearances can be highly deceptive. What made my day was that he patiently signed all the books that I had carried. When he put his signature on *The Great Railway Bazaar*, it was like God signing a copy of the Bible.

And now, imagine my horror, when a fellow passenger, a bearded young man, woke me up to hand me the book.

'It fell from your hands,' he told me.

I had been reading till lunch was served, and after lunch had climbed up the upper bunk to stretch my legs and continue reading. But I fell asleep and the book had fallen off my chest. Fortunately, there was no damage to it.

I climbed down now. Most of my fellow travelers were paralysed by post-lunch laziness. Motionlessly, they stared out of the windows. The train now ran like the animal that had finally found its way out of the confusing terrain and was determined to reunite with its herd well before sunset.

'How long before we reach Guntakal?' I asked the bearded man who had returned my book.

'Thirty minutes,' he said, looking at his watch.

In exactly thirty minutes, the train approached a station called Gooty Junction.

If Ooty stands for Ootacamund, I reasoned, Gooty must be Guntakal. So I put on my floaters and extracted my bag from under the seat.

'I thought you were going to Guntakal,' the bearded man said.

'Yes, isn't this Guntakal?'

'Not yet. Another twenty minutes,' he said. His name was Ahmed and he was a gangman in the railways, posted at Guntakal. I asked him about places to stay in the town, and he named two hotels. 'Both are top class,' he assured me.

A COOL BREEZE SWEPT through Guntakal station when I stepped off the train. It was one of the most pleasant-looking railway stations I had ever set my foot on—clutter-free, crowd-free, standing innocently in the midst of barren lands like a young girl who had been asked by her lover to stay put there till he returned with some ice-cream or popcorn.

For someone used to walking into commotion immediately after stepping out of a train, Guntakal is a huge relief. So old-fashioned is the place that in order to get out of the station, you will have to walk down the platform and cross a railway track by foot to reach the parking area where autorickshaws would be waiting in a queue.

A barricade is put up every time a train is about to

pass, but who wants to wait for the train when all it requires is to look left and then right and quickly cross the track? The onus is on the drivers to be extra cautious while pulling into Guntakal.

I got into an autorickshaw and asked to be taken to one of the hotels recommended by Ahmed. The hotel seemed top class indeed, only that there were no rooms available.

'Is there nothing you can do about it?' I pleaded with the young manager.

'Sorry sir. Only yesterday one party booked all the rooms. It is marriage season, you know,' he replied.

'Not even one room?'

'Sorry sir.'

'Any other good hotel around?' I asked.

He named the other hotel recommended by Ahmed, which was down the road. I walked. At that hotel too, the manager pleaded helplessness. He said he could give me a suite—costing just five hundred and fifty rupees a night— but it was expected to be vacated only by the evening.

Next door was a lodge. I tried my luck there. There too:

'Can I get a room?'

'No sir. All rooms full,' the bespectacled, middle-aged manager informed me.

'Are you sure?' I asked in desperation. I was beginning to panic. It is not funny when, in a town where you don't know a soul, one hotel after another turns you away saying they don't have rooms.

'Yes sir. All rooms full. It is marriage season.'

'Oh, no.' A part of my mind began preparing to return

to the railway station and spend time at the platform until a train to Chennai came along. Another part asked me not to accept defeat at any cost, even if it meant making the platform my home for two nights that I had intended to spend in Guntakal.

'But I have one double-bed. It is AC. You want it?'

'Why didn't you say that before?'

'Only now I realised it has been vacated,' the manager grinned apologetically.

'Okay, how much?'

'Three hundred and fifty rupees per day. Inclusive of taxes.'

My irritation had melted. I now felt grateful.

In the room I changed and turned on the air-conditioner and lay on the bed that had spotless white sheets which gave off the delightful smell of detergent. Precisely fifteen minutes ago, I had been unsure of finding a room in this town. And now I had found paradise. I went to sleep. I had stayed up all night in order to catch the early morning train.

At six-thirty in the evening, after a cup of coffee in the room, I went for a walk on the Station Road, the town's equivalent of Mahatma Gandhi Road.

I had taken the same road while coming from the station, but at the time, perhaps in my eagerness to find a hotel, I had not noticed the shops that flanked the road. In any case, shops look more agreeable and attractive only after sunset: before that, they are like candles burning under sunlight. Right now I noticed them.

They bore signboards such as 'Krishnamurthy & Sons', 'Lingamurthy & Co.', 'Ganga Traders', 'Sivaram Traders'. They still belonged to the era when surnames of the shopkeepers were brands unto themselves. Today, at least in big cities, the roles have reversed drastically: it is the brand name of the goods that keeps the surname of the shopkeeper alive. Only when you sign the slip, generated by the swiping of your credit card, do you notice the name of the firm that runs the shop.

So once again, a brush with the bygone era as I walked, keeping pace with the town that seemed to be in no hurry. Every few metres, there was a phone booth by the road—a yellow phone sitting on a yellow pedestal and protected from the weather by a slanting yellow tin roof. At the first glance, they looked like antique cuckoo clocks. I was not only fascinated by them but also amazed: had these booths been installed in a town in Uttar Pradesh, they would have vanished overnight, uprooted by vandals who would sell them to the scrap dealer for a few hundred rupees. They would sell them not so much for the money as for their instinctive inability to leave unguarded public property untouched. But then, south India is a different planet, in every way.

In the north, for example, you are unlikely to find stationery shops selling posters of Amitabh Bachchan or Shah Rukh Khan. They may sell them on the pavements, but not in proper stationery shops where such posters, considering that cinema is always thought to be distracting and corrupting young minds, would be completely out of sync with the textbooks and notebooks and the pens and pencils. But here, in Guntakal, they proudly displayed posters of Telugu cine icons such as Mahesh Babu, Chiranjeevi, NT Rama Rao, and even Arjun—an actor who has been accorded the title of 'Action King' by his Tamil fans.

One stationery shop was impressively big and crowded and seemed to be selling more than just school textbooks. I walked in. This was a shop for the young men in the town who dreamed of becoming train drivers or station masters. I picked up a book, titled *Kiran's Up-to-date Approach to Psychological Test for Diesel/Electrical Assistant Driver Exams, Assistant Station Master Exams*. On the back cover, it boasted: *For sure success in railway exams, read books published by Kiran Prakashan Pvt. Ltd.*

I wondered why the exams were for the job of only assistant driver and assistant station master. Why not driver and station master? Maybe that's how it works in the railways: you get recruited only at the assistant level, and as the years pass, the prefix gets dropped somewhere along the way.

Flipping through its pages, I felt extremely glad that I had left my days of taking examinations way behind. It is always nice to put your nose into the pages of a book and smell the ink, but the moment you are told that your future depends on that book, the book becomes a burden.

I bought a book that was not as burdensome but at the same time served as Kiran guidebooks' equivalent for every aspiring wordsmith—the *Pocket Oxford English Dictionary*.

I walked on.

All vaccination and injection for dog bite given—announced a clinic that was buzzing with people. I wondered how many of them must have been bitten by dogs.

Then there were footwear shops that sold only Action shoes— remember them? I peeped into one of them: I could have bought half the shop. Okay, that's a gross exaggeration, but you know what I mean. Today, when one has to part with a chunk of one's salary to buy a decent pair of Nike or Adidas, the Action shoes here were a steal. They were not always so, though. One of my prized acquisitions, when I came to live in Delhi in the early 1990s, had been a pair of Action shoes.

Between these shops, there were decrepit buildings that were either no longer in use or shut during the evenings. On the verandahs and steps of these buildings sat the elderly men of the town. These places seemed to be their *adda,* where they met every evening, turned out in their best clothes—starched dhoti, kurta and turban. They didn't seem to have much to say to each other, though. They just sat there, huddled together, watching the town and time pass by.

I stopped at a cosmetics shop. I had remembered to buy a comb. I asked the shopkeeper about the places to see in Guntakal. He said there was a dargah—the tomb of a saint called Syed Mastaan Ali—which attracted a lot of visitors. Then there was a Hanuman temple, about three kilometres away, a very famous one. There was also a church, near the station.

'Any other important place?' I asked.

'Yes, the railway station,' he replied, matter-of-factly. It was understandable that he should treat the railway station as a monument. In the logical scheme of things, you first have a town and then a railway station—just like you buy a whip once you own a horse. But towns like Guntakal, Mughal Sarai and Itarsi came up only after the railways set up their junctions there—the case of buying a horse only because you happen to own a whip.

I sauntered back to my lodge. It was barely eight—too early to go back to my room. I spotted a liquor shop with an attached bar right across the road. I lost no time in walking over.

I was the only one in the bar when I walked in and took a corner table. Within minutes, two elderly men limped in. Each of them must have been over seventy years old. They occupied another corner, right under the poster of a beer company that dared: *Part of a crowd or stand apart? Your call.*

It was sufficiently clear that these two old men were regulars at the bar, the sure-footed manner in which they had limped in. Watching them deliberate over what to order, I tried to imagine the story of their lives. Did these men come here to drink in order to escape the tyranny they suffered at home at the hands of evil daughters-in-law, or were they the kind who unleashed tyranny at home once they got back sufficiently drunk?

It was also possible that the two were childhood friends who met here once a week or so for old time's sake, or maybe they were neighbours who rounded off their evening walk with a drink before they returned home to have dinner and go to sleep. There is no way of telling such things. You can only imagine.

When I turned my attention away from the two men, I found the entire bar suddenly throbbing with life. It had got packed in a matter of minutes. Two men walked up to my table and asked if they could sit with me. I nodded. As if I had a choice.

A small boy, barely ten years old, went from one table to another, selling freshly-fried *vada*s, one rupee a piece. The two men at my table ordered a cheap variety of whisky and sipped it slowly over the *vada*s. They spoke in Telugu, so there was no point eavesdropping on their conversation, but from their body language I could tell that both had had a long day and they were now de-stressing themselves by exchanging notes.

I couldn't resist talking to them. I hadn't had a proper conversation with anyone the whole day. Fortunately, they understood and spoke Hindi sufficiently well.

Both were drivers, employed by people in the real estate business. Whenever their employers or any of their clients came to Guntakal—which could be any day and any time of the day—it was the job of these two men to chauffeur them around. But tonight the coast was clear for them to have a drink. I wondered aloud to them why Guntakal, a tiny town which owed its existence to the railway junction, should have anything to do with the construction business.

'In which world are you living, sir,' one of the drivers, whose name was Ramdas, chided me. 'Land is selling here like gold. Everybody is coming here to buy land, people from Hyderabad, from Bangalore, from Bombay, from everywhere. Just three years ago, one acre of land in Guntakal cost only three lakhs of rupees. Today, it costs more than six lakh of rupees.'

He went on to name a couple of politicians who had recently bought chunks of land in Guntakal, one of them being the daughter of a revered Andhra Pradesh politician.

The other driver, whose name was Balaji, wondered why I chose Guntakal of all places to write a book. I tried explaining to him, but I could see that he had already decided that I was making a mistake.

'If you want to write, write about Adoni,' Balaji said. 'That's the place to write about.'

I had never heard of the place.

'It is in Kurnool district,' he said, 'just a few hours from here. It is a second Bombay. Only millionaires live there. If you go there, you won't feel like coming back. You want to go there? I will take you.'

'Some other time,' I told him. (Adoni, I later learned from Wikipedia, is a town that has a 'substantial textile industry'. Naturally, it must be the home to textile magnates and their opulent lifestyles.)

After that, Balaji sat back and Ramdas did most of the talking. From him I learnt that Bellary—the town in Karnataka where Congress president Sonia Gandhi made her electoral debut in 1999 and defeated Bharatiya Janata Party's Sushma Swaraj with a rather narrow margin of about fifty thousand votes—was only fifty kilometres away. The nearest airport was Puttaparthi, the home of Sathya Sai Baba, one hundred and twenty kilometres away.

After a point we ran out of conversation, and it seemed odd to me that I should return to my shell suddenly after having built up the camaraderie. So I asked Ramdas about his family. He said he had a wife and two children—a six-year-old daughter, and a six-months-old son. He asked me about mine. I told him I had a wife back home.

'That's it? So you hardly have any expenses!' Ramdas exclaimed. 'No wonder you can afford to drink this whisky,' he said, pointing at my quarter-bottle.

There were two things I wanted to tell him: that I had actually taken some money from my wife before boarding the train to Guntakal, just in case I fell short; and that the brand of whisky I was drinking usually invited frowns from many of my friends who, no matter how cash-strapped they are, drink only Scotch whisky. But I let it be.

Suddenly he asked me, 'Sir, what is your salary?'

I was taken aback for a moment. Then I realised that he only wanted to satisfy his curiosity about the kind of money people made in big cities. He would probably never put this question to his employer or the people he drives around, but now that we were sharing the table and having a drink together, he decided to take the liberty, especially since we were talking about money.

When I told him, he sighed. 'I get only two thousand rupees a month,' he said, 'out of that, six hundred goes for rent. I have a wife and two children to support. There are so many expenses. I can't even afford to come here often, even though I would love to. Who doesn't like to have a drink after roaming around like a dog the whole day?'

Balaji, the other driver, who seemed to be cut up with me for not sharing his enthusiasm about the town of Adoni, nodded in agreement.

I offered to buy them a drink each. They refused at first, but relented when I insisted. I needed their company more than they needed the drink.

Ramdas threw another question at me: 'Sir, what is your age?'

'How old do you think I am?' I asked.

'Thirty, or maybe thirty-one?'

'No.'

'Then? Twenty-nine? Twenty-eight? You cannot be less than that. What do you say?' he asked Balaji.

Balaji, still sulking, did not reply.

'How old are you, sir?' Ramdas asked again.

'Thirty-seven,' I replied.

Ramdas looked sad. He said, 'People like you live in AC. That is why you look young.'

I felt flattered. We parted on a happy note. They left, while I stayed on to finish whatever was left in the bottle that I had ordered for them. In their place now sat a man who must have been my age. He looked pensive and avoided eye contact with me. Going by his appearance—a smart striped shirt and matching trousers and not one but five pens in the breast pocket—I gathered that he must be a teacher. Perhaps the right person to shed some light on the town.

'Are you a local?' I asked him, in Hindi.

'Hindi, no,' he replied in English.

I repeated my question in English.

'English, no,' he said, 'Telugu, only Telugu.'

So a conversation was ruled out. It was amply clear that he didn't want any. Still, I thought I must at least see his pens. It is not unusual for a man to carry two pens on his breast pocket, but I had never seen anyone carry five.

'May I see your pens, please?' I asked.

He looked at me blankly.

'Those pens,' I said, pointing at his breast pocket.

He smiled for the first time and plucked one of the pens and uncapped it for me. It turned out to be a voltage tester.

THE SUN WAS BLAZING when I stepped out of the lodge the next morning after a late breakfast of *idli*s and *vada*s and coffee. The night before, I had walked towards the station. This morning, I walked in the opposite direction. In that heat, impoverished hawkers sat by the road, selling limestone chips, while shopkeepers sat glumly at the counters of the deserted shops, reading the newspaper and hoping that a customer would show up sooner than later.

I had barely walked for a few minutes when the row of shops flanking the Station Road terminated into a vast expanse of agricultural land and a clear grey-blue sky overhead. So that was it. It was pointless to walk further.

On a cloudy day, the scenery that lay in front of me might have served as an excellent backdrop for a Telugu song. But right now it was too hot to enjoy the sight. Fortunately, there was an autorickshaw stand right there and I walked up to it. I asked to be taken to the dargah of Syed Mastaan Ali Baba.

The drivers, who were huddled together in a discussion which they clearly didn't want to be distracted from, ignored me at first. But seeing me still standing there, each one passed the burden of taking a passenger— that was me—to the other.

'You take him.'

'No, no, you take him.'

'OK, what about you?'

'Who? Me? No way. Why don't you take him?'

The drivers argued while I stood there, under the scorching sun, waiting for them to make up their mind. Finally, one of them, who looked like a ruffian and their leader, quoted a steep fare by Guntakal standards: seventy rupees. I readily agreed. He had no choice now but to order one of his boys to take me to the dargah.

One of the easiest things in this world is to strike a friendship with a driver in a small town. It may not be always easy to do so in a big city where the drivers, as the saying goes, would have seen hundreds like you. But in a small town, friendships can be forged within moments. All you need to do is ask the driver his name and where he hails from and if he is married. You'll get enough material to write a novella.

If you listen to his story patiently and make sympathetic noises wherever required, you've earned his loyalty. He will go the extra mile for you. Just like my driver Venkat was doing now. Until ten minutes ago, he was a faceless driver, huddled with his companions at the autorickshaw stand. Now he had taken it upon himself to help me make the most of my visit to Guntakal.

He planned a rough itinerary for me as he navigated the lanes and byways, occasionally applying the brake to let a goat pass. Within minutes we had left the morning bustle of the town behind and were now driving through barren lands where vegetation was as sparse as the inhabitation. We wouldn't have travelled more than three kilometres but it seemed as if we had been on the road for hours.

The dargah was deserted when we arrived there. There was, of course, the small band of alms-seekers at the entrance. I ignored them and we walked through an empty courtyard to the tomb of Syed Mastaan Ali Baba. This was one of the most peaceful places I had ever come across: one could only hear the chirping of birds, perched on the tall trees that shaded the dargah. One of the young caretakers, sitting alongside a donation box on a tall wooden platform erected in front of the tomb, took me for a devotee and immediately assumed a solemn air. But when I introduced myself and told him the purpose of my visit, he became excited and started answering my questions to the best of his knowledge.

From what I learned from him, the dargah was 372 years old, and more Hindus visited it than Muslims—from childless couples to people whose businesses were not doing well.

'They come from all over the country. They come from Cuddapah, Nandyal, Kurnool, Bombay, Hyderabad, Bangalore, even your Chennai,' he said. Seeing me taking notes, an elderly woman walked up to me and politely told me that if I wanted authentic information about the dargah, I should talk to Abdul Wahab *saahab*. He was a senior member of the eleventh generation of caretakers of the tomb.

'Where can I meet him?' I asked the lady.

She pointed to a bunch of houses behind the tomb.

'Wait, I will send for him,' she said. A boy ran in that direction.

Abdul Wahab arrived a few minutes later. A mat was quickly spread under a tree and water and sweets were sent for. We took our places on the mat and the interview began.

Abdul Wahab, greying and genial, wore a shy smile, as if he would have preferred to be left alone. But as the conversation progressed, he became more like a father telling a story to his son.

He was now telling me the story of Syed Mastaan Ali Baba. Nearly four hundred years ago, Mastaan Ali had wandered into Guntakal to preach Islam, especially among Edagas, the toddy-tapping class. He had been provided with hospitality by the family of Nagi Reddy, one of the biggest landlords in the area.

One day, the preacher was found with boils all over his body, and the Reddys, fearing that the disease might spread, left him in the jungles outside the village. That night it rained heavily, and the Reddys were suddenly overcome by guilt for having left a sick man at the mercy of nature. The following morning they had rushed to the spot, and found Mastaan Ali completely cured of the boils and looking vibrant.

They fell at his feet and sought forgiveness, and ever since then the Reddy clan has been his devotees. Even today, when processions are taken out from the tomb in the honour of the preacher, the horses are sent by the Reddys and symbolically pulled by the members of the family.

'Without the Reddys, the procession cannot be taken out. They also bear the entire expenditure of the procession. You have missed it by just fifteen days. You should have been here then. There was no place to stand, so crowded it was,' Abdul Wahab said.

Apart from holding a job that has been handed down the generations, Abdul Wahab is also a civil contractor and owns flour mills. In other words, he was not badly off. I asked him about Guntakal. He said the place has had its share of ups and downs.

'I was born in 1944. At the time this place was a village. I remember that in 1955, when I was in class six, there were only three schools here: the SJP School, the municipal school and the railway school. There was no college. Today there are colleges and even private schools where they give you good education. But at the same time, the mill has closed down, the sleeper factory has closed down,' he said.

Sleepers are the rectangular concrete plates on which rail tracks are placed—something I had not known until then. Guntakal, being a hub of the railways, manufactured sleepers until recently but the factory had now closed down. So had the cotton mill which, as I learned later in the evening from the receptionist at the lodge, happened to be Asia's first cooperative mill inaugurated by none other than Jawaharlal Nehru, in 1954. In both cases, troublesome labour unions seemed to have been the culprit.

I was given a fond farewell at the tomb. The elderly woman, who had suggested I speak to Abdul Wahab, came to me and pressed a parcel and sweets and flowers into my hands. 'You have his blessings,' she said.

I got into the autorickshaw and Venkat, the driver, took his seat.

'Why not finish with the visit to the Hanuman temple today?' Venkat asked me.

'Yes why not? But how much extra will you charge?' I asked.

'Give me whatever you want,' he laughed. 'Don't embarrass me by talking about money.'

So off we were, back into the goat-infested lanes and alleys before we hit another road that led to the temple. In one of those lanes, we passed a school that had the 'Thought for the day' written out on a blackboard at the entrance: *'There is no achievement without goles.'* Had I been running that school, I would have fired the English teacher.

The road we had hit now was undulating and tearing through a monotony of barrenness that was occasionally broken by mountains of quarried stones.

'Come here after ten or twelve years, you will find big buildings in this place,' Venkat said, looking at the emptiness around. 'People are buying land here. All big, big politicians, big, big film stars.' He was corroborating what the two drivers I had met in the bar the night before had told me.

For long we kept driving into nothingness, to the point that I began to lose my patience and wondered if Venkat was deliberately taking a circuitous route. That was highly unlikely, though, in a small town such as this, which didn't have too many roads for a driver to take profitable diversions.

I realised my fears were unfounded when an arch-gate showed up, and soon we were within the temple boundaries. I deposited my floaters at a flower shop, bought some flowers and walked on a scalding cement floor into the compound. At that time of the day, when the sun happened to be merciless, and considering that it was not a Tuesday, the day of Lord Hanuman, the son of the wind god, the temple was deserted and I found myself ample space and privacy to sit in a corner and meditate.

Once the mind was at peace, the throat realised it was somewhat thirsty. So when I came out of the temple, I bought a chilled bottle of Bisleri water from one of the numerous shops that dot the compound. Enjoying the feel of the moisture-coated bottle in my hand, I got into the autorickshaw and asked Venkat to return to the town. I lit a cigarette and sat back to enjoy the return journey. Return journeys are always shorter and more assuring.

After I finished the cigarette, I proceeded to open the water bottle and realised that the cap had been resealed. The heated filament used to reseal the bottle had left black marks between the cap and the thread. I held the bottle against the light and took a close look: there were tiny particles floating in the water. I had been conned, right inside a temple.

When I brought it to the notice of Venkat, he suggested that we return. But I let it be. It was pointless to go all the way back for the sake of twelve rupees that I had spent on the bottle. Moreover, by now, we were already back in the middle of nowhere, and it made more sense to invoke the curse of Lord Hanuman on the cheats and keep heading towards the town. I flung the bottle out, and could hear the thud as it landed by the road.

Back in the lodge, I paid Venkat one hundred and fifty rupees and we exchanged phone numbers. He was extremely pleased. I went up to my room and ordered an Andhra meal for lunch.

Andhra meals are famous for their portions: one meal can easily be shared between two gluttons or four diet-conscious diners. Sadly, the meal is not allowed to be shared if you are eating in a restaurant. And sadly, in the lodge, there was no one to share it with me.

The room boy walked in with a gigantic multi-tier tiffin carrier. Just when I was wondering how to cope with so much of food I realized the tiffin carrier contained only the side dishes. The rice came in a steel bucket, which the boy was holding in the other hand. Steam erupted from the bucket as he placed it on the table and removed the plantain leaf covering the mountain of rice.

The food was all mine—something that could last seven days but something that I had to finish within an hour so that the room boy could come and collect the lunch carrier and the steel bucket.

IN THE EVENING, I once again strolled down Station Road and decided to walk right up to the station. On the way, when I was closer to the station, I walked into St Ann's church, said to be dating back to 1880. But the impressive structure I stood in front of now was built, as I learned from the plaque, only in 2002—too recent to look for the romance of the bygone era. In any case, there was nobody there to enlighten me about its history. The church, like the dargah and the Hanuman temple, was deserted. There was a watchman, but he knew nothing. Either Guntakal is a desolate town, which was likely, or my timing at these places was horribly wrong, which was even more likely.

The station was just a stone's throw away, literally, so to prolong the walk, I took a detour by turning into the first street that came my way. Then came another street, and then another. They were all deserted, wrapped in the silence of mourners. It was barely six o' clock, but it seemed like midnight: the silence occasionally broken by boys zipping past in bikes.

What lifted my spirits was the sight of the old railway quarters—cottages left behind from the British era and, thankfully, still intact. They were the modest version of old-fashioned bungalows and were separated from each other by spaces big enough to accommodate a cricket pitch.

Each house had a large garden protected by a wicker gate: Ah! What a pleasant return to the days of *Julie,* the landmark 1975 film about the life of an Anglo-Indian girl who falls in love with and loses her virginity to a Hindu— a Bengali—boy living in the neighbourhood. The inimitable Om Prakash, who had the enviable power of making you laugh as well as cry, plays Julie's father—an alcoholic train driver. The role of the Bengali boy's father is played by the equally inimitable Utpal Dutt.

The film lives on even today, especially in its songs. Passing by these cottages in Guntakal, it was very easy to imagine one of them belonging to Julie: I could almost visualise Om Prakash returning from work and opening the wicker gate and then opening a bottle of whisky.

Later I was to regret not having knocked at the doors of one of those houses to find out if a Julie still lived there.

But right now, walking on the street, I found it inappropriate to call on a family that did not expect me, and therefore headed for the station. I bought a platform ticket and walked over to the platform that housed the offices of the men who ran the station.

As I stood in the office of the station manager, waiting for him to lift his head from the papers he was busy scribbling on, a homily caught my eye:

> *Duties can be taught but not the responsibilities.*
> *—Station Manager, Guntakal*

It was nailed to a panel that bore multi-coloured switches. On these switches, I presumed, depended the safe running of trains passing through Guntakal. In that sense, this room was as important as the cockpit of an aircraft. A minor malfunction can cost the lives of hundreds.

When the station manager finally lifted his head from the paperwork and looked at me inquisitively, I introduced myself. I thought he would invite me to sit next to him and maybe even call for coffee.

But he didn't even ask me to sit, even though I had

been standing behind a vacant chair all this while. He dismissed me outright, though politely, saying I must approach the divisional manager for any information regarding the station.

'We are not authorised to talk, you must speak to the DRM. He will tell you everything, A to Z,' he said. DRM stood for the divisional railway manager.

I stayed put. 'But sir, I am asking for general information, such as …'

'No, no, I cannot give you any information. You must speak to the DRM. He will tell you everything, A to Z,' he repeated.

'But sir, all I want to know is …'

'No, no, I cannot give you any information. You must speak to the DRM. He will tell you everything, A to Z.'

I ended up spending half an hour with him, during which he told me almost everything I had wanted to know about Guntakal station, except that he kept punctuating his sentences with the lines, 'No, no, I cannot give you any information. You must speak to the DRM. He will tell you everything, A to Z.'

During the brief conversation I had with him, I learned that Guntakal is the transit point for the export of iron ore that came from Bellary. At this station, iron ore is dispatched to Chennai and to Kakinada in Andhra Pradesh, from where they are shipped to countries like Japan. I also learned that Guntakal handles nearly sixty trains a day, and that there were five station managers, working on rotation in eight-hour shifts, to attend to these trains.

'It is a highly stressful job. The worst part is dealing with the public. Whenever there is a problem, for example, if a train in running late, they come straight to the station manager because they do not trust any other official. So this is a job that comes with a lot of responsibility and stress,' he said.

I also learned that the station manager, now in his late forties, hailed from Bangalore and had spent nearly all his life in that city before his job with the railways brought him to Andhra Pradesh. 'There was a time when people from Bangalore going to Bombay or Calcutta or Delhi had to first come to Guntakal. During my younger days, I have spent hours at this station waiting for the connecting train to Bombay,' he said.

He must have never imagined that he would be managing the station someday. When I thanked him and took leave of him, I found him almost ready to say, 'No, no, I cannot give you any information. You must speak to the DRM. He will tell you everything, A to Z.'

When I walked out of the station, none of the waiting autorickshaw drivers approached me. They knew it was pointless to spend their energies on a man who was strolling out of the station without luggage. I walked past them, and walked all the way back to the lodge.

THE RECEPTIONIST SMILED AT ME, for the first time, as I walked in. He was chatting with a stocky, elderly man who wore a white shirt and a crisp white dhoti. They stopped their conversation upon seeing me.

'Where all did you go, sir?' the receptionist asked me.

I told him.

'When will the article appear, sir?' he asked. I was too

tired to explain that I was writing a book and not just an article, so I gave him a tentative date.

At this point the dhoti-clad man stepped forward and extended his hand. 'Sir, myself R Moorthy.'

His handshake was firm and I was mildly surprised when I subsequently learned that he was seventy-two. I did not think him to be more than sixty. He too lived in Chennai and was in the business of dyes and chemicals. Since his business was spread in all the four southern states, he often came to Guntakal, which was equidistant from most of the important south Indian cities, in order to stay in touch with the dealers.

'I have been coming here since 1961-62. At that time Guntakal was only a village. Today there is some improvement. For example, earlier there used to be a small bus stand, but today it has become a big junction. But overall, it still remains a village when you compare it with Chennai or Hyderabad,' Moorthy said.

I asked the receptionist how long had he been living in Guntakal.

'All my life, sir. I belong to this place only,' he smiled benignly.

'You never thought of moving to a big city?'

'Where can I go, sir? I am fifty-six now. My life is over.'

'Not now, but when you were younger?'

'No, sir. I was the eldest son. I had to stay here. My younger brothers went away.'

'And what were you doing?'

'I was working in the mill, sir. It was Asia's first cooperative mill. It was inaugurated by Nehru himself. I joined in 1978, as an acting staff [a daily-wager]. There were two thousand workers in all. It was a big mill, built over sixty-two acres. But it closed down in 1991.'

'Why?'

'Same problem, sir. Trade union fighting with management. Today, most of the workers have become labourers. What else can they do?'

Compared to his brethren, the receptionist was not so badly off. His two children were 'well-settled'— the daughter happily married in Kurnool, and the son working for a top television channel in Hyderabad.

'This is a small, peaceful place, sir. Why should I leave it? Muslims form 40 per cent of the population, yet we never had any communal problems. We live like brothers. The only problem was water. There was a time when drinking water used to come only once in seven days. Do you remember, sir?' he asked Moorthy.

Moorthy nodded.

'But now that problem also is solved. We get regular water.'

Back in my room, I switched on the air-conditioner and filled ink in my fountain pen and sat down to write. But not before I had sent the boy to get me a quarter-bottle of whisky and Hyderabadi mutton *biryani*. I can relish meat only after I've had a few drinks, when I am anesthetic to the fact that I am eating a living creature that had just been killed. When I am sober, I resist eating meat, unless it is done so well that I can't tell whether it's mutton or jackfruit.

The room boy returned with bad news.

'*Biryani* finished, sir. All selling. Famous shop, sir. All buying, buying,' he waved his hands to denote a large crowd at the shop.

'Any other shop?'

'Other shops no good. This shop best,' he said.

I had no choice now but to settle for the standard fare of rotis and a vegetable curry. My last night in Guntakal was drawing to a close.

THE NEXT MORNING, after a breakfast of *idlis* and extremely spicy *sambar* at an eatery on Station Road, I called Venkat, the autorickshaw driver. I had a train to catch in a few hours, and there was enough time to visit the mill.

Since I hail from Kanpur, mills—or their closure—were not new to me. My city, once known as the Manchester of the East, has plenty of skeletons as souvenirs from its glorious past—mills built on acres and acres of land that are locked up behind formidable boundary walls. And that includes the 1876-built Cawnpore Woollen Mills, which once manufactured the famous Lal Imli brand of woollen products.

Until some years ago, it was common to see, outside their imposing gates, a group of trade unionists camping there permanently, holding placards and banners that demanded payment of pending wages to the workers. The cloth banners would often be old and faded. When I started my career as a journalist in early 1993, a part of my duty was to translate the press releases sent out by these trade unions. Save the date and the name of the union on the letterhead, the press releases, often handwritten in Hindi, would be similar in style and content. During the past decade, however, the demands-ridden press release died a quiet death. No one knows when exactly it died, but it breathed its last one fine morning when people woke up to swanky malls and the 'imported' brands that had been out of their reach all this while. And no one mourned the death, not even the workers who once took pride in drafting it: they knew their time was up, so they moved on.

Venkat arrived at the appointed time. He seemed extremely glad that I had cared to remember him and call him. So off we were to the Andhra Cooperative Spinning Mills Ltd, a factory that was once the pride of Guntakal, located on national highway number 63 that connects Nellore with Ankola. Nellore is a small town on the eastern coast, in Andhra Pradesh, while Ankola is a small town on the western coast, in Karnataka. Guntakal, lying on the border of the two states, is the mid-point.

At the gate of the mill we were confronted by the watchman. He was the typical watchman, someone I could not imagine doing any other job—silver-haired, tanned face, his drooping shoulders carrying the burden of bad times, yet his eyes shining with loyalty in memory of the good times. He wouldn't let us in.

Venkat pleaded with him on my behalf, telling him that I was an important person who had come all the way from Chennai to write about his mill, but the watchman would not budge.

He could have easily let us in, considering that there was not a soul in the compound other than him to notice the trespassing. But rules were rules, he said. His superiors had instructed him not to let any outsider in, and he was doing his duty.

'This is a highway. You never know who is passing by. If someone sees you walking in, I will be the one to lose my job. You people will go back,' he expressed his helplessness in a friendly way.

He wouldn't give out his name, for the fear that what I would write might cost him his job. But he shared every other information about himself. He hailed from the nearby town of Urokonda and had joined the mill in 1970. He had joined as a daily-wager, getting four rupees a day. After three years, he became a 'permanent' employee. He had put in twenty-one years of service when the mill closed down in 1991. By then, his salary worked out to seventy-five rupees a day. Being a watchman, he did not lose his job, because in troubled times, people like him are required to be around even more. In 1995, the mill applied for loan from a bank in order to settle its dues. The manager of the bank, who would visit the mill often at the time, took a liking for the watchman and asked him to join the bank. He had joined the bank and worked there for a few years until he realised that he belonged to the mill. He was back, even though salary was uncertain. Sometimes he got a bulk payment of two thousand rupees, sometimes five thousand.

Since April 2007, however—that is eleven months now—he had not received any salary. And there were seven other watchmen like him. They worked in three shifts—seven in the morning to three in the afternoon, three to eleven in the night, and eleven to seven in the morning—but they were not getting paid. The hope that the mill management would not let them down and eventually pay them some money, kept them going.

I wanted to ask him how he got his daily bread, and just when I was considering how to put that question in a manner so as not to embarrass him or hurt him, a fellow watchman arrived with a tall, steel lunch-carrier. Indian hospitality suddenly took over. Pointing to the guard-room at the gate, he asked us if we would like to share the lunch. Till a moment ago, we were outsiders, rather intruders, while he was the guard. But now we had become the guests and he the host. He left us outside the gate and went in. Perhaps he was very hungry.

After he excused himself, I saw various unpleasant notices pasted on the wall. One was from the recovery department of the employees' provident fund office, which had fixed 13 March 2008 (less than a month away from my day of visit) as the date of sale for some of the mill property in order to recover nearly a crore of rupees that the management owed the employees as provident fund. Another notice declared that a certain part of the property was under pledge to the Andhra Bank.

Jawaharlal Nehru would never have imagined that his socialist dream would turn out to be a nightmare for lakhs of workers across the country in less than three decades of his death. As a child, I had been witness to some of these nightmares:

Barely two kilometres from our house was a mill called the J.K. Rayon. The tall chimneys of the mill, the sound of the hooter at the beginning and end of every shift, workers trooping across the playground in front of our house in groups while on their way to the mill or way home—these were landmarks of my childhood.

In that playground we played cricket during winter afternoons—the neighbourhood boys, irrespective of which school they went to. Someone owned the bat, someone contributed the ball, and someone else brought the stumps. Pads and gloves were a luxury and largely unnecessary. The umpiring would be done by someone who had finished batting for the day, even though his decisions would often be overruled by the 'third umpire'—one of the neighbourhood 'uncles' closely following the game standing at the gate of his house. It was at this playground that I first met Raja. He was about my age, which was around twelve at that time, and he studied in a Hindi-medium school, which wasn't—and still isn't—a matter of great pride. His father worked in J.K. Rayon, most likely as a lower-rung employee, considering that Raja wore the same shirt for weeks, maybe months. We never got around to becoming friends, but there were times when we would chat after the sun had set. Deep in my heart, I envied him, and maybe even hated him, for being a good bowler. Then one day, J.K. Rayon closed down. I was fourteen then, studying in the ninth standard. The closure was sudden, because only a year before, when we were in the eighth standard, we—as students—had been taken on a guided tour of J.K Rayon so that we got an idea how a mill functions. Suddenly, the hooters stopped calling. Workers no longer trooped across the playground. I myself was at a crucial stage of my life then: board exams were barely a year away, and I had started taking tuitions to strengthen my grip on mathematics and physics. Every morning I would wake up at five and walk to the tuition master's home, which was not very far. But in winter mornings, under the blanket of darkness and dense fog, it would be a challenge to navigate even half a kilometre of familiar territory. Worse, there were street dogs to contend with. On the way back, however, there would be daylight and the fog would have cleared a little. It was on one of these mornings that I noticed, on the same playground, a familiar figure emerging out of the fog on a bicycle. He was calling out, in a lyrical manner, '*Andey*! Double *roti*!' '*Andey*' is eggs, while 'double *roti*', in Hindi, means bread. To protect himself against the biting cold, he was wearing a muffler and a pair of woollen gloves, and his bicycle had a large tin box saddled to it. '*Andey*! Double *roti*!' he called again. It was Raja. Our eyes met, but he looked away, as if he did not know me. Subsequently, I tried not crossing his path while on my way back from the tuition classes, but he was always there, desperately trying to sell bread and eggs to families that were just waking up on a chilly morning to prepare for breakfast. After a point, he did not matter to me, neither did I to him. He had become a seasoned hawker. He was no longer the bowler I envied. All this, because the mill his father worked in had closed down. Since he was the most able-bodied in the family, it had fallen upon him to sell bread in order to earn the daily bread.

Multiply the case of Raja by thousands and you get the picture of India that has failed. Guntakal, too, fitted into that frame. I could see the watchman sitting next to Raja during the photo-op. I have always wondered if there would have been trade unions or calls for strikes, had this been a woman's and not a man's world. Had managements and trade unions been headed by women, I am sure they would have arrived at a mutual compromise during stand-offs to ensure that the kitchen fires kept burning. Women rarely talk big or raise slogans: they are always in touch with what you call the ground reality.

Twenty years ago, I would not have had the luxury of standing outside the gate of the mill and poring over the various notices. I would have been swept aside by an army of workers rushing out to have lunch. But right now, I could only see powerless ghosts of those workers dancing around me. 'Let's go,' I told Venkat, the driver.

BACK IN TOWN, VENKAT dropped me in front of the lodge.

'How much do I pay you?' I asked him.

'Whatever you wish to, sir.'

I took out a fifty-rupee note and two ten-rupee notes and gave it to him, waiting to see his reaction. If he smiled and said, 'Thank you', I would not bother paying him more, and if he didn't, I would give him a couple of tenners more. Precisely at that point, a strong hand gripped Venkat's wrist.

'Seventy rupees? An autorickshaw driver in Guntakal getting seventy rupees?' the owner of that strong hand cried in amazement. Venkat smiled sheepishly and asked the man to let go of his wrist. The man looked at me.

'Do you know what a big favour you have done him? He must have done some good deed in his previous birth to get a passenger like you,' he told me.

Venkat kept up the uncomfortable smile. He obviously knew the man.

I sought to brush him aside by saying, 'Don't worry, Venkat is a friend.'

'Friend?' the man broke into demon-like laughter. Then, letting go of Venkat's wrist, he disappeared into the afternoon crowd on the Station Road.

'What a strange man,' I thought to myself as I watched him fade away. I turned around to ask Venkat who he was. But Venkat was gone too.

TOUCH AND GO
ARAKKONAM AND JOLARPETTAI

THE FRAGRANCE OF THE SOAP from that morning's shower was still fresh when I arrived at Arakkonam junction. It had taken me just an hour from Chennai.

But the scent evaporated minutes after I stepped out in the scorching sun to look for a hotel. All fingers pointed to the direction of a particular hotel near the bus terminus. Perhaps that was the only hotel in the town.

I walked towards my destination rather cheerlessly. Unlike Itarsi or Guntakal, which fascinate you with their quaintness, Arakkonam bore no signs of having matured in the vineyard of time. It resembled any characterless suburb of Chennai—which it is, in a remote sense—where ugly concrete structures had sprung up overnight to accommodate the spillover from the city's population. While strolling through the streets of Guntakal was like sipping vintage wine on a pleasant evening, walking through Arakkonam was like drinking rum on a hot afternoon.

Presumption and conclusion are two railway stations that are miles apart. Yet there are times when we mistake one for the other. The blunder dawns upon us only after the train has left.

I should have merely presumed that Arakkonam, being one of the important gateways to south India, must be enchanting in its own way to hold my interest for two nights. But I had made the mistake of arriving at a conclusion to that effect and budgeted for a three-night stay in a town where I now did not feel like staying beyond an hour.

I found the hotel without difficulty. I climbed up a steep staircase that terminated at a small reception desk. It was unmanned. As I waited for someone to show up, I noticed that the door of the room right across the desk was wide open. There were two men inside: one of them, elderly and dhoti-clad, looked like a prosperous businessman. He was sitting cross-legged on the bed, enjoying his lunch. The other man, much younger and dressed in a white shirt and black trousers, was busy making calculations on a piece of paper. They didn't notice me watching them.

After a few minutes, the elderly man, having finished his lunch, walked out. Lifting his shirt, he adjusted the belt that secured his dhoti and took his seat behind the desk. Only then did he look at me.

'Yes?' He sounded more like a stern headmaster than a hotel manager.

'Can I get a room?'

'AC or non-AC?'

'AC.'

'Five hundred rupees, please.'

I paid.

'Please wait for five minutes,' he said, and called out the other man who was still in that room making calculations. He commanded him, in Tamil, to quickly prepare the room for me. The younger man scurried around like a rat, first smoothening out the bed that until a few minutes ago had served as a lunch table, and then removing the used dishes. The room was ready for occupancy.

I shut the door and sat on the bed. For a while I pondered and then tossed a coin: heads I stay, tails I would leave right away. Heads it was, and I lit up a cigarette to come to terms with the idea of staying there. I reached for the ashtray and discovered that it was already filled to the brim with cigarette butts. I held myself back from being overcome by disgust and decided to enjoy the smoke.

Reclining on the bed and thinking of nothing in particular, I could not help noticing the walls: they were dirty and seemed to be giving off a stench. And then my eyes fell on the numerous used toothpicks stuffed between the mattress and the edge of the bed. It was clear that the manager who, given his girth and landlord-like aggression, was probably the owner as well and considered his guests no better than cattle.

What pinched me was that I had just shelled out five hundred bucks only to invite nausea. In the lodge in Guntakal, I had paid only three hundred and fifty rupees per night for an air-conditioned room, and that was five-star compared to where I found myself now.

But then, I reasoned with myself, I didn't have to spend the whole day sitting in this room. I had things to do, such as go out and talk to people and look for stories, and also visit the naval base, which boasts of an airstrip that is supposed to be one of the longest in the world. According to a former Navy commander I had met in Chennai, the fighter jets that fly past the Republic Day parade in New Delhi take off from that airstrip in Arakkonam: they tear through the skies to fly over the Vindhyas and back in a matter of minutes.

I had come to Arakkonam armed with the phone number of a Navy officer who happened to be a friend of a friend. I expected him to invite me for a drink and regale me with stories about Arakkonam's connection with the defence forces. But now I desperately hoped that he would invite me to stay with him.

'What are you doing in that goddamn hotel, man? Just crash out here'—that's the sort of thing I wanted to hear. But when I called him, his wife answered the call. She informed me, very apologetically, that he was at work and that she would tell him about my call when he came home for lunch.

So I went down to have my lunch. The ground floor of the hotel had a 'meals-ready' restaurant. In that packed eatery, I had a south Indian meal, sharing the table with a tramp whose left hand was tied up in a blood-soaked bandage. Suffice it to say that I finished the meal without the urge to throw up overcoming me even once. After discovering the used toothpicks tucked under the mattress, nothing could perturb me now. I ordered a Limca to wash down the meal and went back to my room.

I called the Navy officer again. The wife answered the call. 'I'm so sorry,' she said, 'he just called up to say he can't make it for lunch. He is busy with some training programme. He said he will call you once he's back.'

'No problem at all. I shall wait for his call. And thank you so much,' I said.

'Not at all, you are most welcome,' she said.

So there was still a faint hope that I might be called upon to be the guest of a Navy officer. But what would I do till I got his call? I decided to roam around the streets, the heat be damned.

So I went to the bathroom to freshen up before stepping out, and that's when I changed my mind irreversibly. Inside the bathroom, there were fresh, slushy footprints that led to the commode. The slush would have been understandable had it been raining, but the weather was as hot and dry as a brick just out of the kiln. The toilet seat meanwhile, was broken and it lay on the floor, waiting to be lifted by someone and placed where it belonged. I was certainly not going to be that someone.

I picked up my bag and walked out. There was nobody at the reception to give a piece of my mind to or inform that I was checking out. No one followed me either, to ask me why I was leaving or to plead with me to stay on. I headed straight for the station. At five hundred rupees for barely an hour, this turned out to be my costliest hotel stay ever.

I had an air-conditioned-class ticket from Arakkonam to Jolarpettai, my next destination. But that was valid for a train that would come only forty-eight hours from now. And since I had booked it online, the cancellation also had to be done online.

So I bought a 'general' ticket, valid only for the unreserved class. That's the only ticket you can buy inside a railway station. Your fate hangs in the balance till the train arrives, when you run across the platform looking for the ticket examiner, who will then take a call on whether you can be allotted a berth against a vacancy, if there is one.

I was lucky here. I made friends with the clerk who issued me the ticket, and who used whatever little influence he wielded to get me a seat in the train when it came a few hours later. I spent that time in his company. He was a young man from Bihar who cursed his posting in Tamil Nadu, and he was more than happy to find a Hindi-speaking companion.

He didn't have much to do at the station, except deal with the occasional passenger who strayed in to make a query or buy a ticket, and make announcements over the PA system about the status of the incoming trains. He would do the announcement first in Tamil, then Hindi and finally in English. I wondered if any of the Tamilians followed his Tamil.

IT WAS EIGHT IN THE EVENING when I reached Jolarpettai, or Jolarpet, the midway mark between Chennai and Bangalore and a key junction for all trains headed for Karnataka, Kerala and southern Tamil Nadu.

Since R.K. Narayan, the writer, travelled frequently between Madras and Mysore, Jolarpettai (Narayan called it Jalarpet) finds a passing mention in one of the short stories contained in *Malgudi Days*. A cool breeze swept through the station as I got down from the train—the only one to do so from my compartment—and walked towards the overbridge.

From the bridge, I could see a brightly lit road flanked by rows of parked Ambassador cars. Just when I was about to climb down the steps, my eyes fell on a notice board: it was a warning from the police cautioning travellers against pickpockets and about snatching of valuables. Precisely at that moment, power went off. Though the lights at the station flickered back to life within a fraction of a second, the Ambassador-lined road that had been visible to me so far was now plunged in darkness.

I instantly reached for my hip-pocket, where I keep my wallet, and mentally prepared myself against a possible attempt to snatch my belongings. But nothing happened. I walked down the stairs and out into the darkness of a road that was lit up only by the whiteness of the Ambassador cars. They were all taxis. I was determined not to ask their drivers—or anyone else, for that matter—about finding a hotel in Jolarpettai. So I walked on.

In the darkness, it was impossible to distinguish one building from the other. I could see only candles burning in each of them. I decided to try out a safe option: I went to a cigarette shop, lit a cigarette, took a few drags and asked the shopkeeper, as if making a casual query, if there were any hotels around. He named two hotels.

I walked up and down the road, trying to locate these hotels, but in vain. Nowhere in the darkness could I spot a silhouette that seemed to belong to a hotel. I started asking around. To my disappointment, both these hotels turned out to be eateries.

'But I am looking for a hotel where I can stay,' I told the man at one of these eateries when he tried to usher me in.

'No hotels here, sir,' he said.

'No hotels?'

'No.' He was no longer interested in me. My heart sank. Where was I to go?

Fortunately, my anxious moments ended at a junction further down the road, where a multi-storeyed lodge appeared, as if by magic. The reception was lit up by a generator. I walked in and introduced myself. I was instantly allotted a room, but was advised to sit at the reception till power came back.

It was a routine power cut, and the supply, I was told, would be back in half an hour. As I waited, I ran my eyes around. On one of the walls hung a picture of Sonia Gandhi meeting a group of politicians from Tamil Nadu. The picture was taken in 1992, according to the date recorded by the camera, which meant it was less than a year after she was widowed.

'That's our owner,' the receptionist pointed to a man in the frame who, along with a bunch of identical men, could be seen paying obeisance to the wife of their departed leader.

On another wall was painted a warning: 'Alcohol not allowed.' Such cautionary signs often mean the opposite. Needless to say, the first thing I did upon checking into the room was to send the boy for whisky and dinner.

The building was a new construction, as one could tell from the way its walls smelt. The only surprising—and uncomfortable—element was the bathroom. It escaped me why the drainage mesh should be positioned right in the centre of the bathroom. But the bed was comfortable and the sheets clean. I drank my whisky, ate *parathas* and omelette for dinner and fell asleep while watching a documentary on the National Geographic Channel about the war in Iraq.

In the morning, when I stepped out onto the verandah to stretch myself, I saw a brown hill that seemed only an arm's length away. Separating the hill and the hotel were lush green paddy fields, glittering under the morning sun. The cool breeze that swept down the hill made me crave for a hot cup of tea. I went down to look for the boy.

The hill that stood there like a watchman over Jolarpettai belonged to Yelagiri, a small hill station that contributes to Jolarpettai's economy. It is no match for Ooty or Kodaikanal, but, of late, it has been attracting tourists and realtors alike.

Being almost equidistant from Chennai and Bangalore, Yelagiri is an ideal weekend getaway—a barely three hours' drive from either of the cities. I had seen reports about the scramble among the rich—politicians, businessmen, bureaucrats—to buy land in this hitherto unknown hill station. Such reports had made me eager to visit the place before hotels and resorts and busloads of visitors spoiled it. This was my moment. Yelagiri, here I come.

But I needed to see Jolarpettai first—the primary purpose of my trip. So, after breakfast I set out on the same road I had walked up and down the night before. The road began at the lodge and terminated, barely half a kilometre away, at a small railway reservation office. On my left ran the length of the railway junction, and on my right a row of shops and food stalls, and a few houses. That was it. I had seen Jolarpettai in less than twenty minutes.

In all my earlier journeys through Jolarpettai, whenever

my train stopped at the station, I had imagined a busy town waiting outside to be explored someday—a town that was a cross between a suburb of Chennai and a suburb of Bangalore. But out here, there was no town. Only a short stretch of road that catered to the two basic needs of the station crowd—food and drink.

I walked beyond the reservation office, hoping to find the real civilisation of the town. But the road melted into nothingness within a matter of minutes: not a soul in sight even at eleven in the morning. I retraced my steps and walked into the reservation office and asked if I could get a ticket for Chennai that night. The clerk tapped away at the keyboard, scanning through the options I had, but he finally shook his head, 'Sorry sir, no seats.' I walked out in despair.

But what if the real town of Jolarpettai lay on the other side of the railway station? Most railway stations, by default, have two exits—one leads you straight into the bustle of the town, while the other usually opens to a relatively quieter side. Maybe I had been walking on the quieter side all this while.

So I took the overbridge and walked over to the other end, crossing, in the process, the breadth of the magnificent railway junction—so big, so clean and so quiet. Climbing down the stairs, however, I was stopped by an eyeball-to-eyeball confrontation between a monkey and a dog. The monkey was perched on the handrail while the dog had taken position on the stairs. The monkey knew the dog wouldn't be able to reach him, yet he stayed put on the handrail, daring the dog to make the first move. The dog stayed where he was, on high alert, waiting for the monkey to make the first move. Neither took the risk.

Eventually, a group of burqa-clad women, who had been walking ahead of me, found the courage to shoo the dog away. The monkey, having won the battle, leaped on to the asbestos roof of a wagon depot whose signboard proudly proclaimed 'We are marching towards ISO 14000'—an enviable standard in quality control.

This side of the station was in fact what seemed to be a normal town, albeit a very small and quiet one. There were shops, there were houses, and a temple too. It took me precisely ten minutes to walk its length and breadth.

I walked farther and ran into the railway quarters. A large crowd had gathered outside a house. It was obvious that somebody in that house had died and that the funeral had not yet taken place. I stopped there for a while, but ended up inviting curious stares. I walked on, climbed the overbridge and crossed over to the other side where I had lunch at one of the 'meals-ready' hotels.

At the restaurant, my companions were two Tamilians who sat on the table next to me. They were having an argument that was so heated that the food on their table lay ignored for a long time. At times, the way they raised their voices and gesticulated, I feared they would turn violent and one of them might end up dying. Or maybe it was just a friendly bantering fuelled by alcohol: the liquor shop was next door. How I wished I understood their language.

The food, meanwhile, was good: the rice was steaming hot, the sambar fresh and spicy and the ginger-laced buttermilk heavenly. The lunch somewhat lifted my spirits, which had begun to sag at the thought that there was absolutely nothing to write home about Jolarpettai, which had turned out to be merely an extension of the railway platform.

As a town, it sustains itself because of the railway junction and because of its proximity to the townships of Thirupathur, famous for sandalwood craft, and Vaniyambadi and Ambur, both famous for tanneries whose products adorn innumerable pairs of feet in Rome and elsewhere in Europe. All these townships are within a distance of 30 km from Jolarpettai. For residents of Jolarpettai, these prosperous towns are what Bombay would be to a Bhopali.

Upon my return to the lodge, I asked the receptionist to get me a taxi for Yelagiri. My joy knew no bounds at the thought that I would escape the boredom of Jolarpettai by going, of all places, to a hill station, that too a lesser-known one. The less known a hill station, the more stories you can spin to your friends once back in the plains. I had been riveted by stories of Yelagiri ever since a colleague went there a few years ago. He had driven down with his family from Chennai to Jolarpettai and then to Yelagiri in order to spend a quiet New Year's Eve there. For just twelve hundred rupees, he had rented a suite in a respectable hotel. For years after, every time we took a smoke break, he would sing praises of his twenty-four-hour stay there.

So I got into the brand-new Maruti van that had been summoned for me, and prepared for a long trek up the hills. But I was there in twenty-five minutes. That included the five minutes when the driver had paused waiting for an obstinate bunch of monkeys to get out of the way. The drive reminded me of going to Chamundi Hills from Mysore: it takes hardly twenty minutes to get there and hundreds drive up every day to pray to goddess Chamundi. Yet no one is under the illusion that he or she is driving up to the level of a hill station, even though you get a bird's-eye view of royal Mysore from the top, just like Yelagiri now offered a view of Vaniyambadi, the footwear township.

Needless to say, Yelagiri disappointed me. Not just because I had reached too quickly. There was something else too. A hill station, by definition, is a town atop a hill. But for us Indians, a hill station is not hill-station enough unless it bears the stamp of the British Empire. It's the colonial connection that lends the romance, apart from the bone-chilling cold. Yelagiri had neither: it was more like a leafy neighbourhood of Chennai that had been, by some geological miracle, lifted a few hundred feet off the sea level.

The driver asked me where he should take me. I told him I had no idea. So he took me to a lakeside park, which seemed to be the chief attraction of the town.

In spite of all that I had read about the sudden interest being shown in Yelagiri, there was not a soul in sight when I entered the park. Perhaps my timing was horribly wrong. I saw a booth at the entrance where one had to pay a nominal fee to gain entry. But the booth was deserted and I lingered at the entrance for a while hoping that a gatekeeper, who may have gone to get a cup of tea or answer nature's call, would return and ask me to buy a ticket. But no one showed up and I walked in.

I walked straight to the lakeside where, to my pleasant surprise, I found an ice-cream parlour that was functional. I bought a cup of vanilla ice cream and stood by the lake. There was a board that read:

ROEING BOAT
Adalt   Rs 15 (1 No.s)
Childrens Rs 10

The tourism department could do well by hiring a proofreader, especially since it has ambitious plans for Yelagiri. The strange thing is that Yelagiri is being sold to potential tourists with the sole promise that it is not as spoiled as Ooty or Kodaikanal. But is that also not an invitation that says, 'Please come and ruin us, like you ruined Ooty and Kodaikanal'?

A gentle breeze ruffled the surface of the lake glistening under the sun. The boats tied to the bank looked bored. In the absence of any company or spectators, there was no fun taking a ride in them, even if it cost only fifteen rupees an hour. So I finished my ice cream and went into the park, where two couples were rediscovering their childhood on the swings and slides.

I sat on a bench and watched them. They seemed to have slipped away from the view of prying eyes on the plains and escaped to the hills to spend the afternoon. Frolicking in the garden, they looked like characters straight out of a 1970s Hindi or Tamil film. Only that they weren't singing to the accompaniment of an elaborate but invisible orchestra.

In one corner, the gardener had just set a pile of dried leaves on fire. The smoke began to spread and it was time for me to leave.

I woke the driver up. He was not pleased to be woken up. I asked him if there was any other place worth seeing. 'Which place?' he asked. I had no answer to that. He was perhaps one of those drivers who was used to picking up and dropping people at designated places, and not the kind who transformed into a friendly guide as the journey progressed. I got into the car. We began the return journey. I was sure I was missing out on a few places. But never mind.

We were back in Jolarpettai in no time and I asked the driver to drop me at the railway station. Since the station was the liveliest place in the town, I decided to spend some time there without the bother of waiting for a train.

I roamed the platforms for a while and then walked into the station master's office. He and a guard were bending over a table on which rested files and clipboards stacked with sheets of paper. I introduced myself and told them the purpose of my visit. Actually, I was more eager to seek their help in getting me out of the place at the earliest. I was no longer interested in knowing about Jolarpettai, so bored I was.

But it would have been rude to just barge in and ask them to put me on the next train. So I opened my notebook. The station master began explaining me the importance of Jolarpettai as a railway junction:

'This is the convergence point of three important divisions of the railways—Chennai, Salem and Bangalore. This is where the crew changes. This is an important junction for all trains coming from Chennai and going to Kerala or Karnataka.'

I asked him if he had anecdotes to share about his stint at the station. The guard, who had listening to us, spoke up, 'Yes, yes, I remember. There was a major accident at Vaniyambadi in February 1981. I was a guard in a passenger train at the time. There was a collision of three trains, Madras–Trivandrum Mail, Yercaud Express and one goods train. It all happened within seconds. More than two hundred people were killed. I was here, at the station, that evening. All the trains had to be regulated from here.'

While the guard was speaking to me, the station master had quietly slipped out and he presently returned, munching on a *vada*. Another piece of *vada* sat intact on the paper plate on his palm. The freshly-fried *vada* smelt so good that I was tempted to ask him, 'Sir, can I please have that one?' But I ended up asking, 'Sir, can you please help me find a berth in any of the trains to Chennai?'

He looked at his watch and said, 'The next train comes in another hour. Buy a general ticket and get your luggage. I will do what I can.'

'Can I check out of the lodge?'

'Oh yes. Just be here ten minutes before the train comes.'

I HURRIED TO THE LODGE. The very road I had walked in darkness the night before, anxious about finding a place to stay, was now preparing for the evening. Hawkers were spreading their wares on pavement and shoppers were coming out. The place suddenly looked friendly and I felt bad running away like this. Spending one more night in the lodge, drinking and watching TV and savouring the cool breeze sweeping down Yelagiri hills, wouldn't have harmed me. I felt worse when I noticed that one of the hawkers, a crumbling old man, was selling something I can never resist: wood apples.

It would not be an exaggeration to say that if I were given a choice between half-a-dozen ripe wood apples and a bottle of Black Label whisky, I would settle for the former.

Life has strange ways of compensating you. Only days before starting off for this leg of my journey, I had had lunch in Chennai at a restaurant that is shadowed by a large wood-apple tree. I had never noticed the tree before, because I had always come to this place in the darkness of night for dinner. But that afternoon I noticed dozens of greenish-brown wood apples hanging from the tree.

Since the restaurant is located in an upscale area of Chennai, I made no attempt to get them plucked. But nature seemed to have sensed my desire, and one ripe wood apple fell on the road with a thud. I was still looking at it in amazement when the wheel of a passing car crushed it, spraying the entire area with a fruity smell. And now, this old man was selling dozens of them.

If I had my way, I would have bought many of them. But space was a constraint, so I bought only five pieces. I couldn't wait to get back to the lodge. Once in my room, I cracked open one of the wood apples with the lock and scooped the pulp with my fingers. The remaining four I stuffed into the rucksack and came down to the reception to clear the bill.

'You are leaving so soon?' the receptionist asked.

'Yes, some urgent work has come up.'

'Yes, I know. Journalists are busy people.'

'But I am not sure if I will find a seat in the train. In which case, will you keep a room for me?'

'Yes why not?'

At the station, the station master assigned me to one of his assistants. The train came, and the assistant made sure I found a seat. But I breathed easy only after I paid the excess fare to the ticket examiner and ensured that the seat was legally mine.

All I wanted now was to get home quickly so that I could crack open the remaining wood apples.

BY THE BHARATHAPUZHA

SHORANUR

ABOUT HALF A DOZEN PEOPLE reclined around a set of Bose speakers, on which Village People's *YMCA* played with such clarity that I detected sounds I'd never heard before in the song.

Glasses of single malt were being passed around. Everybody relaxed after a hectic day at Kovalam. One of the privileges of being the guest of an army officer is that you don't have to worry about asking for—or getting—a drink.

The host was a recently retired Army officer, who once led soldiers in Kashmir and Sri Lanka but who now lives in a luxurious tenth-storey apartment that overlooks most of Trivandrum. Only that you barely got to see the city because it is camouflaged by Kerala's trademark greenery.

His bar was as grand as his career. The collection of bottles matched the souvenirs and artifacts that you expect to find in the home of a soldier whose ancestors have been in the army ever since the Anglo-Sikh War.

He was in an expansive mood. Apart from the single malt, he plied us— a small bunch of people known to him directly and indirectly but who were equal beneficiaries of his generousness—with anecdotes about Army life.

I asked him if he missed the action, and whether he would accept, maybe, a governor's job, if it was offered to him. He gave a boyish smile. 'I served for forty-four years. I have seen enough power and action. No job excites me now.' Then, raising his glass: 'Now I want to enjoy life.'

It was one of those evenings you wish never ended, but just as I was finishing my second drink, someone pointed to the clock. I had a train to catch in an hour. I was hastily served dinner by the cook. The cook was a Garhwali, but the *appam* and mutton stew he had prepared was so delectable that he would have done Kerala proud in a food festival.

After such a splendid evening, it was highly disappointing to board a second-class coach of Amritha Express that was to take me to Shoranur junction. This was going to be the final leg of my journey. What was taking me there was the fact that Shoranur, for decades, had been the Mughal Sarai of Kerala.

No Malayali could reach Bombay without a halt at Shoranur. Similarly, the journey between Chennai and Mangalore and vice versa would not have been possible without the mandatory long stop at Shoranur where the train got to catch its breath while the passengers filled their stomachs and water bottles.

Time was when but for Shoranur station, Kerala would have remained inaccessible to a majority of fellow Indians. Even today, if you are coming to Kerala from Delhi or

Bombay, you will have to spend a few minutes at Shoranur. Yet, Shoranur is hardly known outside the state. Even within Kerala, it is known primarily as a railway junction. So what is Shoranur, the town, about?

The only thing I knew about it was that it was on the banks of the Bharathapuzha, Kerala's equivalent of the Ganga. Almost every Malayalam poet worth his salt has written at least one poem in praise of the river. And considering that one in every six Malayalis sees a poet when he looks into the mirror every morning, the number of words written in celebration of the Bharathapuzha would far outnumber those written in tribute to the Ganga.

TRIVANDRUM STATION HAD ALREADY retired for the night when I reached there at eleven. The magazine shops were shut. Not even a newspaper to distract me from the discomfort of having to sleep on a bunk without a sheet or a pillow.

I climbed up my berth, set the alarm on the phone—Shoranur was to arrive at five-thirty in the morning—and lay down. The next thing I knew was the train standing at a station and the man on the lower berth mentioning Shoranur. I lowered my head and asked him if we had reached Shoranur. He said yes. I jumped down, strapped my sandals on and, still half-asleep, hopped out of the train.

'Wait a minute,' my sixth sense nudged me, 'something seems to be amiss. Why don't you check again?'

I asked a man passing by if this was Shoranur. He looked at me as if I was drunk. 'This is Thrissur. Shoranur forty minutes more.'

I jumped back into the train. The man who had misled me was now fast asleep—or at least pretending to be. I lay down once again, planning an imaginary itinerary in a place I had no mental image of, except that it would have its share of coconut trees. The only thing I was certain about was that I would be meeting Mr Sankarankutty, an old-time resident of Shoranur, who had been referred to me by a colleague.

An imaginary conversation with Mr Sankarankutty kept playing in my head. Sometimes the conversation would be taking place in the morning, over coffee, and sometimes in the evening, over drinks. In other words, I tried everything possible to keep myself awake for the next forty minutes.

The sun was still in bed when I reached Shoranur. Outside the station, the air was crisp and chilly. I felt like going for a brisk walk. But to where? Under the cover of darkness, a new town was as good as the forests of Amazon. Two buses stood outside the station, their conductors trying to outdo each other in shouting, 'Palghat! Palghat! Palghat!'

I was told to check out a hotel that was right opposite the station. I spotted the hotel but the main building was deep inside a walled compound and the gate was locked. I tried making sounds on the gate but they were not loud enough to catch the attention of the watchman or the caretaker. I gave up and started walking.

By now—thanks to my experiences right from Mughal Sarai to Jolarpettai—I had become 'hotel-hardened'. If at all such an expression were to be coined, it would be defined as 'someone who has overcome the fear of not finding a hotel in a small, strange town.'

Fortunately, I didn't have to walk far. About fifty feet down the road I came to a building outside which a man was noisily using the broom like a sword. The signboard identified it as a hotel-cum-restaurant.

'Can I get a room?' I asked him. He pointed to the entrance and motioned me to go in. Right inside the door was the reception desk on which a lean, bearded man rested his head and was fast asleep. I wondered if there was any point in waking him up if all he had to tell me was that he had no rooms.

'Hello," I woke him up. "Can I get a room?'

He woke up with a start and reached for his glasses. He had not expected a visitor at that hour. 'Single or double?' he asked.

'Anything.'

'I have one room. But there is no TV. Is that okay?'

'Yes, it's okay.' I thanked my stars for having arrived at a time when one room was still vacant. My tired bones were not at all prepared for the 'sorry-sir-no-rooms-available' response. After filling the details in the register, I asked the bearded man if I could get some food. Relieved at having found an accommodation, I was now overcome by hunger. He looked at his watch. 'Now it's 6 o' clock. This place opens only at 8 o' clock,' he said, pointing to the restaurant that was part of the hotel.

From the shape of my room, it seemed the mason had absent-mindedly constructed it as a triangle and then, realising his mistake in the last minute, tried to make a rectangle out of it. But the room was clean and so was the bathroom. I changed and lay on the bed. The battle between hunger and sleep kept me awake, and as soon as the sun rose, I went out in search of food.

A stall outside the station was already feeding its first lot of customers: most of them seemed to be labourers and painters who were stocking up on fuel before a long day. Some were having *puris*, and some *dosas*. I asked for both. The food wasn't great, but it was freshly prepared and I couldn't have asked for more. I finished with a milky glass of coffee.

By now, the grocery shop next door had also raised its shutter. I bought a towel and a couple of Medimix soaps. I wanted a newspaper too, but he sold only Malayalam papers.

Back in the hotel, I asked the bearded man at the reception how far the Bharathapuzha was. 'Hardly a kilometre. Actually less than that,' he said. I decided to check out the river the first thing after I woke up. With my stomach now full, I didn't have to wait long to fall asleep.

I HAD KEPT SOMETHING FROM you all this while. It's a terrible disease I suffer from, which gets worse every time I travel alone. Right from Mughal Sarai, the disease has been my invisible companion. Every time I would feel a minor discomfort in the chest, or numbness in my limbs, it would wickedly whisper into my ear, 'You might be getting a heart attack', or 'It could be the symptom of a stroke.'

When you are all alone in a godforsaken lodge in a small town where the fastest mode of public transport is the cycle rickshaw, it is not at all funny to be told such things. And right now, having woken up after an early breakfast of oily *dosa*s and *puri*s, I felt the same discomfort in the chest.

In my heart of hearts, I knew it was just heartburn, but what if it wasn't? I found myself beginning to be paralysed by panic and had to act while my limbs were still moving. I had to get the antidote to hypochondria as quickly as possible.

I went down and asked the bearded man at the reception if he could send someone to get me a quarter-bottle of whisky. He refused outright, saying his boys were not supposed to fetch alcohol. But he was kind enough to tell me that the shop was hardly two kilometres away and that it should not be too much of a problem for me to get it myself.

I was about to step out of the hotel to look for an autorickshaw when I got a call. The caller turned out to be Sankarankutty, the old Shoranur hand whom I had been recommended to meet. He asked me where I was staying. I told him.

'Can I come over?' he asked, very benignly.

'Sure, sir. Can we meet in an hour?'

'Oh yes. It is 10.30 now. I shall be there by 11.30. Is that okay?'

'Of course. Would you like to have a drink?'

'No, I don't drink.'

'You don't drink at all or you don't drink in the daytime?'

'No, I don't drink. I will see you at 11.30.'

I could tell that my question had embarrassed him. Now there was a double emergency of making it to the liquor shop. I not only had to go buy a bottle but also gulp a couple of drinks down to cure myself of hypochondria before Mr Sankarankutty arrived. I walked down the road and flagged down an autorickshaw and gave the vaguest destination I've ever given to any autorickshaw driver: 'Wine shop'.

But that's the thing with autorickshaw drivers: he spoke no English, I spoke no Malayalam, still he understood what I meant and off we were to the nearest liquor shop. To get there, we had to cross the Bharathapuzha and turn right into a lane and then into a couple of alleys. I was not at all prepared for this abrupt introduction to the river. I was hoping to run into it at my own pace after an invigorating walk, but right now I was crossing it sitting in an autorickshaw, feeling like a man being rushed to a hospital in an ambulance.

It was 10.30 on a Monday morning, when you expect people to be busy earning their living. But the bar at the liquor shop was packed, as if it was a Saturday evening. It was populated mostly by wiry, bearded men who were downing their drinks with such urgency that it seemed as if they were drinking a bitter medicinal concoction that had to be gulped down in one go. I was no better: I too was visiting a bar on a Monday morning. But in my case, the alcohol was now indeed supposed to be medicinal.

I bought the whisky and got into the waiting autorickshaw. Subsequently, I learned that once you cross the river from Shoranur, you are technically in Thrissur district. So even though I had travelled barely a couple of kilometres, I could boast that I had gone all the way to Thrissur to buy a bottle of whisky.

The driver charged me only fifty rupees. Considering that it had been an alcohol-related trip for him, he could have asked for even eighty or a hundred and I would have still paid him. But this was god's own country where the autorickshaw drivers are an honest lot, irrespective of the god they follow.

Back in the hotel, I sent for a plastic glass and a bottle of water. But before they could arrive, Mr Sankarankutty did. He had a freshly-starched dhoti tied around his lean waist and a Parker pen tucked in his shirt pocket. He was the perfect elderly gentleman—Kerala's version of the Bengali *bhadralok*—extremely soft-spoken and courteous. He had a companion, equally soft-spoken.

Forget the drink, there was no question of even lighting a cigarette in front of him—so proper was he. I felt ashamed about the whisky bottle that now stood like a sore thumb on the side table, but it was too late now to remove it. I pulled out my notebook from the rucksack and sat in front of him like a pupil. Mr Sankarankutty began to speak.

'Shoranur was a small village a hundred years ago. It had no importance. But when South Indian Railway (a company that existed long before Independence) started a long-distance train from Madras to Mangalore, Shoranur happened to be in the middle of the route. That's how it became an important place.

'Then the king of Cochin requested the management of South Indian Railway to extend the service to Cochin as well. That's when Shoranur became an important junction. At that time, some seventy-five years ago, there were more than 3,000 railway employees in this town. There was a loco shed. Small-scale industries grew in the town. Shoranur was famous for cutlery and agricultural implements.

'But now everything is lost. The loco shed is now in Erode, and Palghat has become a divisional office. The importance of Shoranur went down. We did not like it, and political parties agitated against the importance of Shoranur coming down. The government promised to start a coach factory, but it never happened.

'Today we can see trains from Chennai, Bangalore and Delhi going past Shoranur without even touching the station. We only hear their whistles. At least twenty trains don't stop at Shoranur anymore. It is such a tragedy.'

Mr Sankarankutty blamed 'influential politicians' from Tamil Nadu for usurping the important role played by the Shoranur junction and getting them assigned to Erode, a textile town in Tamil Nadu not far from Shoranur. But in the same breath, he also admitted to the fact that labour unions too played their role in the decline of Shoranur as an important railway junction. 'They gave a red mark to Shoranur,' Mr Sankarankutty laughed at his pun.

In Kerala, you can afford to joke about unions only if you are a member of one. It didn't surprise me, therefore, when Mr Sankarankutty told me that he, after retiring as the deputy director of education, was now an office-bearer of the pensioners' union of Kerala, which boasted of three lakh members. And while in service, he had been an office-bearer of the gazetted officer's union of the state.

I was once again overcome by embarrassment that I had actually offered a drink to a retired deputy director of education, that too at ten-thirty in the morning. It was my good luck that he had taken the trouble of coming to the hotel. I assumed he had walked down all the way because he was carrying an umbrella.

Soon after Mr Sankarankutty had arrived, I had run down and asked the man at the reception to arrange for some coffee and biscuits. He obliged me with great alacrity, because he had clearly not expected an elderly Malayali *bhadralok* to call upon a man who, a few minutes ago, was looking for alcohol. He suddenly saw me with great respect now and had rushed one of his boys to do the needful. Presently, the coffee arrived along with biscuits and cake.

Mr Sankarankutty now relaxed over coffee and told me that he had worn other hats too. He had been the secretary of Kerala Kalamandalam, a school for performing arts, for five years. He had also published eight books, covering a wide range of subjects, from interpreting Kathakali, the traditional Kerala dance form, to expounding the 'beauty of mathematics'. He had also written scripts for Doordarshan. He was presently on the editorial board of a publication from Palghat and also the chairman of the local Kendriya Vidyalaya, or Central School.

He said I must visit Kerala Kalamandalam, which was just three kilometres down the road across the river, in Thrissur district. The Kalamandalam, I was told, was founded in 1930 by Vallathol Narayana Menon, the poet laureate of Kerala. It is now a deemed university, which gives degrees in performing arts. I promised him I would visit it.

'But tell me something, why do Bengalis still use surnames that indicate their caste? We used to do it in Kerala fifty years ago, we don't do it any more. But you people still use Mukherjee and Chatterjee and so on.'

I did not have an answer to his question, but I knew that the question was a well-meaning one, asked out of innocent curiosity by one member of the communist society to another presumed member.

By now, I had completely forgotten that a whisky bottle was sitting there. The conversation with him had distracted me from my hypochondria and I felt perfectly fine. After he left, I reached for my skipping rope and jumped five hundred times non-stop. I knew I was in perfect shape to climb a mountain.

FIVE O'CLOCK. Almost twelve hours since I had arrived. I stepped out of the hotel. The lean bearded man, whom I had seen sitting in the reception since early morning, stood outside rather melancholically, watching the sun slowly turn into an orange ball. He smiled at me and we got talking.

His name was Abdul Majid, and the hotel was owned by him and his two brothers. They took turns in sitting at the reception. 'All the three of us used to live in the Gulf, in Jeddah. But when our father died, our mother asked us to come back. You can't live there all your life, can you?' he said.

It was quite likely that the hotel was built with the money the three brothers had earned in the Gulf, but I did not press for details. I was in a hurry to get to the river, fondly called Nila by the locals, before the sun set. I knew the routes by now, which were pretty simple. To my left was the road to the river, and to my right the road to Shoranur town. I started walking left, with a spring in my step. Within a matter of minutes, I was climbing down the steps at the bridge.

The river had shrunk to being a rivulet, leaving open a vast expanse of white sand for visitors and loiterers alike. So this was it—the river that inspired a galaxy of Malayalam poets. I am sure there are months when the Bharathapuzha lives up to its status of an awe-inspiring river, but right now it was an apology of a river whose flow seemed to be powered by poetry rather than physics.

I sat on the sands and smoked a cigarette and watched the green waters flow with quiet determination. I saw no harm in smoking there because the sands were already strewn with, among other things, empty cigarette packets. Cigarettes and communism have always gone hand in hand since there can be no better way of building comradeship than sharing a smoke. I sat there till I could see only the silhouettes of the vehicles passing on the bridge against the fading light. When I got up, I realised I was the only one there. I hurried back, and walking past the hotel, went to the town.

That's one thing about Kerala: the sameness. You may be in a small town like Shoranur or in a quiet neighbourhood of Kochi, certain things are common—wiry, respectable-looking men moving around in white shirts and white *dhoti*s, Ayurvedic pharmacies, stalls that from a distance seem to be selling only plantain and newspapers but which sell practically everything under the sun, from cigarettes to soaps to towels, slogans or banners that constantly remind you that you are in a Marxist state.

The sameness, since it blurs the distinction between

small towns and big towns, is perfectly in sync with the communist character of the state. In other states, especially in north India, a small town invariably means a backward place. In Kerala, there are no such distinctions: even if you go to a remote place, you will still find stalls selling plantain and newspapers as well as wiry, respectable-looking dhoti-clad men going about their work. In other words, being in Shoranur was almost as good as being in Kochi, but being in Mughal Sarai, which is as big or small as Shoranur, did not even remotely give you the feel of being in Lucknow.

I strolled up and down the main road, passing grocery shops, Ayurvedic stores, a couple of churches, one mosque, palatial houses and maybe half a dozen of the plantain-cum-newspaper stalls. I stopped at a couple of them and asked for a newspaper. A whole day had passed and I had no idea what had happened in the rest of the world yesterday and what was going on today. But they kept only Malayalam papers.

Not knowing what to do next, I entered a hair-cutting saloon, which was clearly the biggest in town, if not the only one. But at the moment, I was the only customer and the barber showed me to a chair with a smile.

'Short,' I told him, and he nodded.

After a few minutes, when he must have found it odd that I was not making any conversation, he asked me, 'Malayali?'

'No,' I replied.

'Then?'

'From Chennai.'

'But not Tamil, no?'

'No.'

'Then your native tongue?'

'I'm a Bengali,' I said.

His face lit up. 'Oh Bengali! Bengali, Malayali same thing. Communism, cinema, culture ...' He could have gone on talking, but his English was as limited as my Malayalam. But I could see from his eyes that he was genuinely happy to have me in that chair. I was glad that he did not speak English or else it would have broken his heart to know that I never lived in Bengal and was, culturally, more of a UP-wallah.

I have let down—and even offended—quite a few Malayalis during my visits to Kerala. When they come to know that I am a Bengali, they presume that I hail from Calcutta and that I must be distantly related to Jyoti Basu.

Once, at a small gathering in Trivandrum, where a young man, in order to impress me about his knowledge of Marxist literature emanating from Bengal, had asked me, 'So what do you think of ...?' He named someone I had never heard of.

'I am sorry, but who is he?'

'What? You never read his books?' he was shocked. 'He is such a great writer.'

I told the young man that I had never heard of this writer. He was indignant. 'What? You never heard of him? He is also a Ghosh, then how come?'

'I am sorry, but I have never heard of him.'

'What? You never heard of him? He is one of the leading lights of communism. How can a Bengali not read him?'

I told him I had never lived in Bengal and that the communist movement did not interest me much.

'Oh, so where are you from?'

'I am from Kanpur, in Uttar Pradesh.'

'But your surname says you are a Bengali.'

'Of course I am a Bengali, but born and raised in Uttar Pradesh.'

'Oh, so you are a rootless Bengali. No wonder.' The young man looked smug as if he had won a battle and poured himself another drink. He looked around for approval, fortunately, the other members at the gathering had kept a straight face.

The language barrier prevented a similar conversation at the saloon. It would have been shattering to be called rootless by a barber. I looked at the mirror: the barber was snipping away at the hair of a man who was a mixture of a Bengali, UP-wallah and a Madrasi, who indeed had no fixed roots and was rather glad about it. I paid fifteen rupees for the haircut.

Sporting a new look, I walked back to the hotel. The bottle of whisky I had bought that morning was still lying unopened. I opened it with pride because I had managed to do without it the whole day. I called a Malayali friend in Chennai, and the conversation with him helped me decide my itinerary for the next day. I would be going to Nilambur, a small town two hours away by train. The primary purpose would not be to visit the place, but the journey itself, because the train chugged through teak plantations and green forests. 'You should not miss it at any cost,' the friend in Chennai said.

I WENT TO THE STATION in the morning and bought a ticket. When I saw the fare printed on the ticket—only thirteen rupees—I told the clerk that I wanted a reserved ticket and not a general class ticket. 'Don't worry, all coaches are general. No classes,' he said.

The most worn-out train standing at the station was the one bound for Nilambur. Its coaches were ageing and the seats were wooden. But what mattered to me now was that it was practically empty. Only a sprinkling of passengers in each coach. I took a window seat and opened my notebook.

A Muslim man, attired in a spotless white headgear, white shirt and a dhoti, occupied the seat in front of me. His wealth showed in his Rolex watch and the mobile phone which he kept pressed to his ear for most of the journey.

No sooner had the train moved out of Shoranur than the trademark green of Kerala changed shades. Instead of the regular coconut trees, we were cutting through teak plantations. Each tree had a number carved out on the trunk: 317, 318, 319 and so on. Every now and then, an opulent house, newly built in Islamic style, would spring up from amid the greenery.

The train suddenly came to a halt. I thought the engine had developed a snag, so I headed to the door to get down and breathe the fresh air. Suddenly, with a jerk, the train began to move. It was a scheduled halt, at a small station called Kulukkallur—so small that it could have been a bus stand.

The route was dotted with small stations such as this, where you heard nothing but silence and saw nothing but greenery for miles around. I suddenly envied the job of the station masters at these places. Maybe, they would have envied mine. Angadippuram was the only station that was big and chaotic enough to look like a regular railway station. The Rolex man got down there. Soon after the train pulled out of it, the air turned chilly and hills, covered in blue haze, appeared on the horizon.

Then came Pattikad station, which presented me with a sight I had never seen before: a woman emerging from a small asbestos-roofed room carrying the signalman's green flag and waving it at the train. Melattur is another station I am not going to forget easily: it was right in the middle of the forest and as soon as the train pulled in, the air seemed to have been sprayed with a strong citrus smell.

Finally, Nilambur—a small pretty station right in the lap of nature. It looked more like an assembly point for people setting out on a jungle safari. I wondered if a town could exist in a place like this, but there seemed to one, considering that the giant clock at the station read, 'donated by Lion's Club of Nilambur'.

I asked a vendor when the next train was back to Shoranur. 'Seven o' clock,' he said. No train before that? I asked. 'Yes, this one,' he said, pointing to the train that had just brought me. It was going to start its return journey in ten minutes. I dropped the idea of going out and made the most of my ten-minute stay at the station by settling on a bench with a packet of biscuits and mango juice.

WE SAT UNDER THE STARS and sipped our drinks. Girish was a friend's friend. I had first met him six years ago, and we were meeting for the second time now. When he was told that I was here, he had decided to drive down thirty kilometres from Palghat to spend an evening with me.

By now, after living out of the bag for several weeks and drinking in dingy bars with masons and drivers for company, I had forgotten what it was to be served by a liveried waiter who asked you questions like, 'Soda or water?' or 'Ice or no ice?'

It was a delight to be sitting on the lawns of The River Retreat, a heritage resort built on the banks of the Bharathapuzha. Drumbeats and firecrackers could be heard at a distance, and every now and then, sparklers would light up the skyline.

'Is there a festival today?' I asked Girish.

'Every other day is a festival here,' he laughed.

The river, which shimmered under the burst of sparklers, looked almost like a roadside puddle formed by a spell of rain.

'Look what have they done to it. Sand mining has changed the character of this river. Now you have grass growing on its bed,' Girish sighed. Till then, I had no idea that he had grown up in Shoranur, in a house not very far from where we were sitting.

'We call it Nila. The bed used to be sandy. Very fine sand. Whenever I would be stressed over something, I would come here and lie on the sands. During my college days, we used to play cricket on the river bed. But now it's all spoiled. All because of sand mining,' he sighed again.

Maybe he was right. Or maybe that he had outgrown the romance of the white sands, now that he had a job to keep and a family to look after. Having last seen him seven years ago, I could notice the transformation. Back then, he was skinny, lounging around in a vest at a discreet drinking session on the sidelines of my friend's wedding. Now he had grown a paunch and acquired an expensive car.

When the bill came, he insisted on paying. I would have none of it: he had, after all, come all the way to give me company. When I paid, I realised that two hours at the lawn had cost me more than what I had spent in two days in Shoranur.

The next day, I had to take the train back to Chennai at noon. But I was yet to visit Kerala Kalamandalam. I set the alarm for seven in the morning and went to bed. I could still hear drumbeats and cracker bursts at a distance.

IT TOOK ME BARELY ten minutes to reach the Kalamandalam, which is a residential school that believes in the *guru–shishya* tradition and which imparts training in performing arts of Kerala such as Kathakali, Koodiyattam, Mohiniyattam and Panchavaadyam.

Throughout the way, I had tried imagining the sights that were likely to greet me. The only image that I could see was a sprawling campus on the banks of Bharathapuzha, where students in small groups practised Kathakali, dressed in masks and costumes. Would they be distracted if I stood there and watched them, I kept asking myself. I needn't have worried.

When I reached the Kalamandalam, walking up the steps under the gaze of its founder Vallathol Narayana Menon, whose statue looms large over the sprawling compound, I found people, mostly clad in white, huddled in small groups. An uneasy silence hung in the air.

I approached one of the groups and introduced myself. I was told that there would not be any classes today because a Kathakali artiste guru had died. He was fifty-eight years old and had died of complications caused by heavy drinking. In any case, classes weren't happening at the moment because the students were busy with their exams—the regular exams that called for skills in science and mathematics. I asked them if I could take a walk around. Most welcome, I was told.

So I started walking around the main building. The backyard was dotted with a number of hut-like structures made of bricks. Each of these was big enough to accommodate about twenty students, and this is where the dance classes are conducted. These huts were presently empty. Most of the students seemed to be in the hostel or in the canteen, which seemed to be the only noisy place on a campus that otherwise maintained a dignified silence.

In one of these huts, however, there were about half a dozen boys huddled together over slim workbooks. Wearing innocence on their faces and white dhotis around their waists, they made the picture-perfect *shishya*s. They must not have been more than twelve years old, and they began to giggle and hide behind each other when I approached them. They were so shy that conversation became impossible. All I could gather was they were studying for their English exams.

The ice was broken only when I asked them which

sport they liked the most. 'Cricket!' they replied in unison. And which kind of dance did they learn here? 'Kathakali!' again in unison.

But they quickly retreated into silence when I asked them to show me a few steps. Once again, they began to hide behind one another. After much goading, one boy began to demonstrate some eye movements, which are very crucial in Kathakali. But the others began giggling and the boy, overcome by shyness, terminated his performance in a matter of seconds.

In the end it all ended well. They were as curious about me as I was about them. They wanted to see what I was jotting down in the notebook, they examined my pen, asked me where I came from and what I did. All this in broken English. I asked similar questions and they began to talk, about their favourite cricketers and favourite actors. Finally, when I shook their hands before leaving, they insisted that I stay on for a while. I told them I had a train to catch.

On the way back to the hotel, I crossed the Bharathapuzha river once again, for the last time. I wouldn't have paid much attention to the fact that this was the last time I was crossing it—at least for now—if not for the fact that the river was synonymous with creativity. So I took one last good look at it as soon as the autorickshaw driver hit the bridge, hoping that the sight would pump up my creative juices as well.

Back in the hotel, as I collected my belongings and put them into the rucksack, I realised that I badly wanted to stay on for a couple of days more. I wanted to take the ride to Nilambur once again, and also wanted to spend an entire afternoon sitting on the sands of Bharathapuzha.

But then, as they say, time and tide—and let me also include the train—wait for none.

I HAD, BY NOW, travelled about half the breadth and almost the entire length of the country. If I were to join with a pencil the towns I had visited during the past few months, I would be drawing a crude 'S' on the map of India.

These are towns that don't mean a thing to you because you never get down there, but at the same time they mean the world to you because no train journey is complete without them. They are irrelevant, yet they are a ritual.

Next time when my train halts at any of these junctions, my mind would be racing back to the lanes and the byways of these towns, which I know now like the back of my hand. But since I have been there and done that, I would, in all probability, be standing at the door of my coach and looking out for the man calling, *'Chai, chai!'*

ACKNOWLEDGEMENTS

The writing of this book required me to do little except take the train and record my impressions of the places I travelled to. As a result, the list of people I need to thank for helping me in my endeavour is embarrassingly short. Since the number of people is few, each of them gets a generous dose of my gratitude. The recipients are:

Gautam Padmanabhan, for showing faith;

Sushila Ravindranath, my ex-boss. Without her prodding this book would have just remained an idea;

Navneet Kohli, Mangesh Yadav, Laxman Jaiswal and Rajeev Srivastava, for being friends in strange places;

Rohit, my brother, for making life easier in Itarsi;

Shuvashree, my wife, for running a comb through every chapter;

Anubhuti Krishna, Charmaine Edwards and Meenakshi Kumar, for going through the draft and making valuable suggestions;

and M.T. Saju, a loyal friend. Countless evenings with him gave me the courage and confidence to proceed from thinking about writing a book to actually writing one.